BLACK AMERICA, BODY BEAUTIFUL

BLACK AMERICA, BODY BEAUTIFUL

HOW THE AFRICAN AMERICAN IMAGE IS CHANGING FASHION, FITNESS, AND OTHER INDUSTRIES

ERIC J. BAILEY

Foreword by Cynthia Warrick

Westport, Connecticut
London

Library of Congress Cataloging-in-Publication Data

Bailey, Eric J., 1958–
    Black America, body beautiful : how the African American image is changing fashion, fit-
ness, and other industries / Eric J. Bailey ; foreword by Cynthia Warrick.
        p. cm.
    Includes bibliographical references and index.
    ISBN 978-0-275-99595-9 (alk. paper)
    1. African Americans—Psychology. 2. Body image—Social aspects—United States.
3. Beauty, Personal—Social aspects—United States. 4. Consumers' preferences—United
States. 5. Industries—Social aspects—United States. I. Title. II. Title: African American
image is changing fashion, fitness, and other industries.
    E185.625.B325   2008
    155.8'496073—dc22   2008007993

British Library Cataloguing in Publication Data is available.

Library of Congress Catalog Card Number: 2008007993
ISBN: 978-0-275-99595-9

First published in 2008

Praeger Publishers, 88 Post Road West, Westport, CT 06881
An imprint of Greenwood Publishing Group, Inc.
www.praeger.com

Printed in the United States of America

The paper used in this book complies with the
Permanent Paper Standard issued by the National
Information Standards Organization (Z39.48-1984).

10 9 8 7 6 5 4 3 2 1

DEDICATION

This book is dedicated to my grandmother, Lula Ballew. Lula Ballew is my mother's (Jean) mother, and, together with her husband, my grandfather John Ballew, she raised five daughters (Jean, Thelma, Ophelia, Arnetta, and Lulu) and one son (Johnny). In writing this book, I often thought of my grandmother Lula Ballew, primarily because she was a beautician who owned her own beauty shop in Wyoming, Ohio, for a number of years during the 1960s and 1970s. What I remember most about her are the months my family—mom, dad (Roger), brother (Dwight), and I—lived with her and Granddad. I was starting fifth grade. We moved in with them because we had moved to Wyoming in 1969 and were looking for a place to rent. Well, during those months of waiting, I saw my grandma work practically every day in her beauty shop that was connected to her house. It was an eye-opening experience and something I never forgot.

She was a very assertive, organized, independent, and beautiful woman who ran her beauty shop like an assembly line. Not only did I see her wash, cut, dry, and style other black women's hair, I also saw her give these women their own type of beauty when their hair was done. After doing so many heads by the end of the day, my grandma would get tired. I can't tell you how often I saw her fall asleep in her favorite chair in the family room with her feet on the footrest, wearing her white beautician's outfit. That is the image that has stuck in my head for years, and in writing this book, that is the image that returned to me. I was, and still am, so proud of my grandma Lula Ballew.

CONTENTS

Foreword by Cynthia Warrick   ix

Preface   xi

Acknowledgments   xv

1. The Impact and Importance of Body Image and Body Types   1

2. Race and Body Image   7

3. Body Image Preferences among African Americans   23

4. Cultural Historical Review of Preferred Body Images and Body Types   35

5. African American Body Types and the Fashion Industry   49

6. African American Images and the Advertising Industry   61

7. African American Body Images and the Fitness Industry   71

8. African American Image in the Television and Movie Industries   83

9. African American Image and Politics   105

10. Global Perspective: How Are African American Images Viewed by Other Countries?   117

11. Conclusion   125

Notes   133

Selected Bibliography   149

Index   151

FOREWORD

African American concepts of beauty and physical appearance have been formed by cultural, environmental, and socioeconomic factors. In the early 1600s, Africans were brought to the North American continent, ushering in the institution of race-based slavery. The more than 100 years of oppression influenced African Americans' views of beauty, which were intricately linked with their survival. The mass media and commerce gave currency to such adages as "white is right" and "if you're black, get back," and promoted the straightening of hair and the merchandising of skin-lightening products and makeup, as well as toys, games, and dolls. The black power movement of the 1960s helped to instill a sense of racial pride and self-esteem in American blacks, leading to replacement of the name "negro" with "black" and to acknowledgment of African heritage.

I am a product of the transforming views of African American society. Growing up in South Texas, I lived in a segregated community and attended an all-black school through the second grade. My ideas of beauty were of course influenced by the views of my mother, whose favorite actress was Dorothy Dandridge and favorite performers were Nancy Wilson and Johnny Mathis. My own views of body image were influenced by my dolls: Chatty Cathy, Barbie, and Tressy—all white, and the latter two shapely with long, blond hair. When Twiggy became the first teenage supermodel in the 1960s, I donned apparel of the mod fashion—bold-patterned mini-dresses and above-the-knee go-go boots, even though in junior high my dress size was 13. I was so embarrassed to have developed breasts that I slumped in an effort to hide "them," despite my mother's constant reminders to hold my shoulders back. I also enjoyed watching the Miss America and Miss Universe beauty pageants that showcased the ideals of mainstream beauty and talent.

By the time I was in high school, the civil rights and black power movements were full blown, and I quickly adopted the Afro hairstyle, signifying pride in my black identity. Although the Afro was "the look" of the 1970s and through all my years in college, I found it was not acceptable in the mainstream workplace, where I would earn the distinction of being the first and the only African American in most of my employment positions. Throughout these years, however, my perception of body image continued to be influenced by my mother, formerly a physical education major and dancer, and by my profession and my friends, who were all very conscious of their weight. We are all confident, educated African American women, and are sensitive about our body size as it relates to our health and appearance. However, our ideals of beauty have changed—ranging from skinny Twiggy of the 1960s to today's full-figured Queen Latifah. Recent *American Idol* winners and finalists also reflect a fuller body image, as epitomized by Ruben Studdard, Jennifer Hudson, and Jordin Sparks.

As a health care professional and academic, my research focuses on the health disparities among African Americans. Eric Bailey's book fills the void of scientific evidence to enhance the understanding of African Americans' perceptions related to body image and beauty. Few studies have presented a comprehensive approach to this subject, and Dr. Bailey is the first to document these issues from the perspective of the African American male.

Cynthia Warrick, PhD, RPh
Dean, School of Math, Science & Technology
Elizabeth City State University
Elizabeth City, NC

PREFACE

Black America, Body Beautiful: How African American Image Is Changing Fashion, Fitness, and Other Industries is a book about a people's struggle to find their particular preference for body image and recognize that their body images, body types, and standard of beauty are greatly influencing today's fashion, fitness, and entertainment industries. This cultural journey, as it relates to body images, body types, and standard of beauty for African Americans, challenges not only mainstream America's standards but also the perceived standards within the African American community.

Before I sat down to research and write this book, I asked myself two straightforward questions: Why I am interested in this topic of body image? Why am I, as an African American man, writing this book? Even though I knew the answers, they made me slow down and contemplate what issues I wanted to discuss and how I could investigate these very sensitive cultural topics in a professional manner.

I am interested in body image as it relates to the African American populations in the United States and to people in other countries primarily because of the dearth of research and discussion of it in the popular media and particularly in academia. Oftentimes, individuals, African American or otherwise, feel uncomfortable investigating and talking about the physical and cultural images associated with African American body types. Throughout our history, these images have been presented as stereotypes, thereby negatively influencing people's perceptions of African Americans. Even today with the latest media technologies, such as iPods, the streaming of videos to computers, and the hundreds of cable and satellite stations, the African American physical and cultural images regularly seen by most mainstream American audiences, as well as African Americans, are very limited and stereotypical. Fortunately, to date, a number of renowned individuals from diverse fields have provided a better appreciation and understanding of African American body images, and this book recognizes their contribution to this very complex cultural issue.

I am also interested in this topic as an active and athletic African American man; I have always been curious about how I developed my preference for a particular body image. What were the major factors that influenced my striving for that "ideal" African American male body? Furthermore, I wanted to know the major factors that may have influenced my perceptions of an "ideal" African American woman's body, and why they were similar to those of other African American men. These issues, although discussed among friends and family, are seldom investigated.

Chapter 1 starts the dialogue and debate of the impact and importance of African American body images and body types upon several key industries in the United States, such as those related to fashion, fitness, advertising, modeling, and entertainment. This chapter contends that a cultural revolution has been occurring in these industries, and it highlights commentary from media outlets, celebrities, Web blogs, and surveys to support that assertion.

Chapter 2 confronts the issues of race and body image and investigates to what degree all of us are influenced by our ethnicity in our preference for certain body images. This chapter highlights several research studies investigating ethnicity and body image preference as well as how our individual enculturation process may influence our preferences. Studies highlighting the enculturation process among European Americans, Hispanic/Latinos, Asian and Pacific Islanders, and Native American and Alaska Natives in relationship to their preferred body images are presented.

Chapter 3 focuses specifically on the preferred body images of African Americans. The chapter highlights the positive feedback that I received from African American audiences when I presented data from my previous book examining the health issues related to body image. Research studies conducted within several African American populations are presented as quantitative and qualitative evidence for how African Americans perceive their preferred body images and body types and how they are different from and similar to other ethnic groups.

Chapter 4 examines the cultural and historical factors that may have influenced people's perceptions of African American body images and body types. The physical and visual imagery of African Americans through various periods, as seen through European American and African American perspectives, are presented here. Examining the cultural impact of the early years of African American hair practices and beauty contests helps us better understand how these cultural issues significantly shaped the overall body types and images of African Americans.

Chapter 5 examines the relationship of African Americans to the fashion industry. African Americans have had a very long history in the fashion industry since its inception. They have always organized and presented their own style and fashion shows throughout the African American communities in the United States. This chapter highlights those early years of accomplishments as well as the entry of African Americans into mainstream fashion industry. Renowned African American fashion models such as Naomi Sims and Tyra Banks are discussed.

Chapter 6 focuses on the advertising industry's use of African American images to sell and promote various products in America. Historically, African Americans have had to endure the advertisement industry's use of blatant stereotypical imagery to sell products. This chapter recognizes those experiences and also highlights how the advertising industry has dramatically changed to present positive imagery of African Americans. Examples of celebrities such as Mo'Nique, Raven Symone, Queen Latifah, and Oprah Winfrey are presented to highlight this significant change.

Chapter 7 encourages the fitness industry to improve its physical imagery and connection with the average African American. This chapter highlights how more segments of the fitness industry, such as the health-and-fitness book publishers and clubs, are implementing African American initiatives in their programs and thereby improving the overall body images associated with the population. This chapter also discusses the significant contributions of well-known athletes such as Venus Williams, Serena Williams, and Tiger Woods in their attempt to change the physical imagery of African Americans within the fitness industry.

Chapter 8 examines historically the early images of African Americans in the television and movie industries and shows how much those images have changed in the mainstream as well as the African American media. This chapter highlights the contributions of pioneering actors and actresses such as Paul Robeson, Hattie McDaniel, Lena Horne, and Sidney Poitier. It also recognizes the black filmmaking industry and its pioneers such as Oscar Micheaux, Melvin Van Peebles, Gordon Park, and Spike Lee, who have introduced a diversity of black physical imagery to both African American as well as mainstream audiences. Finally, this chapter challenges those audiences to further expand their perceptions and dispel their misconceptions on how African Americans should look, talk, and behave on television or at the movie theatre.

Chapter 9 examines the sociocultural historical issues connected to the image of African Americans in politics. A brief historical review of the major African American political movements is presented and how they influenced mainstream American politics, as well as an analysis of the contemporary issues of African Americans in politics. This chapter highlights the significant impact of Barack Obama and Condoleezza Rice to the overall image of today's politics.

Chapter 10 focuses on the global perspective and how other countries view African Americans. An analysis of a research study is presented as well as personal accounts from African Americans living and visiting other countries in the world. Interestingly, the types of images that many countries associate with African Americans are quite limiting and stereotypical. The major reason for these types of stereotypical images associated with African Americans in other countries are directly connected to the types of images that our mainstream media exports to these countries on a daily basis through television, movies, and the entertainment industries.

Finally, Chapter 11 summarizes the major reasons why I wrote this book, and it provides evidence of America's changing body image standards. This chapter provides several action-oriented and culturally competent approaches in changing some of the misconceptions and stereotypes associated with African American body images, body types, and culture. National private-industry campaigns such as *My Black is Beautiful* and the *Campaign for Real Beauty,* along with fifty years of *The Ebony Fashion Fair—The World's Largest Traveling Fashion Show,* are prime examples heralding the arrival of a cultural revolution.

ACKNOWLEDGMENTS

This is my fourth book with Greenwood Publishing, and it has been one fantastic journey in learning more about the publishing industry and about me. I want to sincerely thank my remarkable editor, Debora Carvalko, for working with me on another book project.

Now that I have established myself back in academia, I want to thank both of the academic departments in which I am jointly-appointed at East Carolina University—the Anthropology Department and the Masters of Public Health Program of the Department of Family Medicine in the Brody School of Medicine. The support from both departments and schools (Thomas Harriot College of Arts and Sciences and the Brody School of Medicine, has enabled me to expand my perspectives and expertise in research, teaching, and service for the university and the community at large. In addition, I want to thank the two outstanding libraries at East Carolina University—The William E. Laupus Health Sciences Library and the J.Y. Joyner Library—for their excellent research journals and book collections as well as the outstanding administrative staff there.

Along with the research in libraries, there is also fieldwork. I want to thank the Ebony Fashion Fair Show for visiting Greensboro, North Carolina, so that my wife and I could witness the glamorous fashions for women and men as well as experience this unique cultural event. In the writing of this book, I have to acknowledge the motivating, uplifting, and soulful music of Vanessa L. Williams, the first African American to be crowned Miss America, and Chaka Khan, the undisputed Diva of Soul, R&B, and Funk music.

Fortunately, I have had a number of key scholars who have supported my career throughout my years in academia and at the National Institutes of

Health. They are Richard Levinson, Rick Ward, Bernice Kaplan, Madeleine Leininger, Mark Weiss, Jim Hamill, George Fathauer, and Edward Sharples.

As always, I pay my ultimate respect to all of my immediate and extended family members, past and present (aunts, uncles, and cousins)—especially my incredible, determined, and beautiful mother, Jean Ethel Bailey; father, Roger Bailey; and brothers, Dwight, Ronnie, Billie, and Michael Bailey. I thank them for their guidance

Finally, I want to thank my understanding, supportive, and growing family for putting up with late-night writing, music playing, and numerous hobbies—my very beautiful wife and co-host on podcast shows, Gloria; my daughter, Ebony; and my sons, Darrien and Marcus.

—— CHAPTER 1 ——

THE IMPACT AND IMPORTANCE OF BODY IMAGE AND BODY TYPES

INTRODUCTION

A cultural revolution has been taking place in the fitness, fashion, advertising, modeling, and broadcast industries. Outsiders may not have noticed it yet, but to people who work in or are affiliated with these industries, it is obvious. This revolution is impacting all of us in so many ways. African American body images and body types are revolutionizing fitness, fashion, advertising, modeling, and television programs as well as movie content. The following examples provide evidence of the revolution.

The Sports Apparel Industry

In 2005, Nike, an international sports apparel and shoe company, launched a brand-new marketing campaign that celebrated the physical fitness and curvaceous body shape of a woman of color. The campaign received international attention from media and customers because the ads simply showed a woman's rounded backside in short shorts. This photo caused a major fury and intense discussion in the sporting, advertising, and fitness industries and among the general public.

Here is a sample of some of the comments about this Nike campaign, found in business journal and third age blog forums:

What a nice ad. It's good to see healthy, thick women that are appreciated. I applaud Nike and Dove and any other company that purports this image. Hail to and celebrate the beauty of the body.

Wow! Now that's what my husband calls a "classic booty," the kind [for which] black women have been celebrated for generations. In the African American community, a butt like that is considered the epitome of feminine beauty. Fancy that—the black aesthetic making inroads into "mainstream culture."

The only way for a marketer to succeed is to think like the consumer. That's exactly what the Nike marketers are doing by using that butt to get consumer attention. They must have realized how much attention the consumer pays to the healthy African-looking booty.

I think there is something beautiful to celebrate in every culture. Every race and culture has features about them that are beautiful. I think, as a black woman, we have been told to cover up our butts, because they were too sexual. There is nothing wrong with having curves. I think that this is a very strong move for Nike. I am glad they're doing it.

Well allow me to add my comment on the black men. I can't really speak for white America, but it is no mystery that the picture in the Nike ad is euphoria for black men and Latino men and by and large men of color. Is it fair to only to portray one body type in the media like we usually see [Men] like curves[, and isn't] that what defines a woman[,] her beautiful curves? It's about time we see real women and what really appeals to men. Enough of the stick figures. This picture to me is ideal female beauty.

I love how people always ignore the fact that the ideal body type in African American culture does not come without work. The ideal is curvy, not fat or out of shape. Black men want a woman with a small waist, wide hips, and a round bottom. Because a woman has a big behind does NOT mean that she does not work out. In fact, it means the opposite. Anyone who has ever worked on a Stairmaster for more than 2 weeks knows that particular exercise for the lower torso will cause the muscles to expand in that ass-area. Because Nike is running an ad with a big-bottomed woman does not mean that it wants to cater to the out-of-shape masses. That woman does not have a single roll hanging from her waist area.[1]

These ads are right on and brilliant. They will help women overcome the stereotype of exercise bulk. As a runner, I joke about my huge "thunder thighs." In reality, they're not fat, just big and muscular from lots of squats last year. This campaign lines right up with what I am learning in my Sports and Society class. Yes, the thunder thighs aren't fat ones, but muscular and yes, the butt isn't a ghetto booty, but to some women with thighs, shoulders, knees, legs, hips, and butts like the ones depicted in the ads, this will go a long way in helping with their self-confidence and realizing it's okay to be muscular. They don't have to look like the super-skinny (sometimes due to an eating disorder) fashion models and movie stars. Yea for Nike! Ads like this make me glad Nike is my school's sponsor.[2]

These blog comments reveal a strong visual admiration, sensual association, and cultural connection to a woman's curvaceous buttocks and hips. Are these public comments on a Web site sincere, and do they have any impact on other industries targeting the African American population?

People responded very favorably to Nike's advertisement. With such strong support for the campaign, particularly in the African American community, a number of other key industries have taken notice.

The Clothing Industry

For example, the clothing industry that manufactures jeans and slacks for women has recognized the public's interest. One new company, Apple Bottoms, has designed their new line of jeans specifically for women with fuller hips.

Apple Bottoms is a clothing line that caters to fashion-forward women of all shapes and sizes. It's their mission to celebrate and liberate the natural curves of a woman's body, and the company's designs concentrate on accentuating these features. This unique brand is the brainchild of multiplatinum recording artist Nelly. The superstar rapper describes the intent behind the designs by saying, "The clothes should fit a woman, not the woman fit the clothes" (www.applebottoms.com/company.asp).[3]

Nelly is personally involved in the design process to make sure that the fashions deliver the magic to reveal the beauty of the woman who wears them. In addition to their jeans, the Apple Bottoms line now includes casual wear, club wear, and even "Golf Glam" wear.

Celebrity customers of Apple Bottoms include Vivica A. Fox, Alicia Keys, and Oprah Winfrey. In fact, on Winfrey's Web site for her show *Oprah*, in the section on "Oprah's Favorite Things—Holiday 2004," Ms. Winfrey listed "Apple Bottoms Jeans by Nelly" as one of her top twenty-one holiday gifts.[4]

Whether it is the impact of Apple Bottoms jeans or just the clothing industry waking up to women's preferences for better-fitting jeans for curvier shapes, other fashion companies have taken notice. For example, Spiegel—one of the largest international fashion and furniture companies, which started selling women's apparel to mainstream America in 1912—is now promoting a new line of apparel and shapewear called Shape Fx. Shape Fx clothing is "designed to make the body you have look like the body you want."[5]

According to Spiegel's advertisement, Shape Fx jeans do it all: slim hips and thighs, lift and shape the rear, and hold the wearer in all over. Jeans in this line are available in three flattering fits: boot-cut, classic, and a "curvy fit" that follows natural curves to perfectly accommodate a small waist and full hips. Here is Spiegel's description of their new curvy-fit jeans:

Push-up curvy fit jeans in two-way stretch cotton with Lycra for all-over control any way you move. Our new curvy fit is cut to follow natural curves and perfectly fit a small waist and full hips. Push-up construction lifts and shapes the rear for your most flattering look ever.[5]

With this description of their new curvy jeans, as well as their entire line of Shape Fx jeans, Spiegel has responded to their customers' desire for better-fitting jeans for curvier shapes.

The Fashion Modeling Industry

The influence of African American body images and body types can also be seen in the fashion industry. For example, Barbara Summers's book, *Black and Beautiful: How Women of Color Changed the Fashion Industry* (2001), highlights more than sixty years of black fashion models' triumphs and successes, from Ophelia DeVore in the 1940s to Naomi Campbell and Tyra Banks today.[6] In particular, supermodel Tyra Banks has truly challenged the body types and body images in the fashion industry.

At a time when fashion models were described as being too skinny, Banks's physique stood out at 5' 10" tall with reported measurements of $34^1/_2$–$23^1/_2$–$35^1/_2$. Although these measurements may be considered slender for women in general, in the modeling industry they are considered voluptuous. Banks had to work hard to persuade fashion designers that her physique was well suited to the catwalks. She says:

I was proactive . . . I told my agency to call Victoria's Secret, and I told them to call *Sports Illustrated* . . . I said my body is changing, and seamstresses are calling me *grosso* in Italian, and I know what the hell that means. And I'm not about to starve.[7]

Banks modeled runway shows in Paris, Milan, Tokyo, the United States, and London. She has been featured in a variety of magazines, commercials, and billboards. Her modeling credits include Cover Girl, Swatch, Pepsi, Nike, Tommy Hilfiger, Victoria's Secret, Ralph Lauren, McDonald's, and Dolce & Gabbana. Banks has graced many international fashion magazines, including covers of *Vogue, Elle, Elle Girl, L'Officiel,* and *Sports Illustrated.*

Presently, Ms. Banks hosts two TV shows: *The Tyra Banks Show* and *America's Next Top Model.* In particular, *The Tyra Banks Show* has challenged the societal and cultural issues connected with America's standards of body image and body types. In fact, in November 2007, Ms. Banks premiered two special shows titled "Bodyville I and II," investigating America's obsession with certain body images and body types. Since Ms. Banks is also CEO of her own corporation, Bankable Productions, and has a charity foundation, TZONE, she continues to be a positive, self-empowered role model for all women particularly for younger black women.

The Fitness Industry

African American body images and body types are even changing how Americans view a "physically fit" body type. For years, it has been customary to see muscular African American men's bodies on muscle and fitness magazines, yet it is quite unusual to see African American female bodies on any fitness magazine or book cover. See for yourself: the next time you check out at the grocery store or visit a newsstand or bookstore, look at the front covers of all the major health and fitness magazines; very seldom will there be a female person of color on the cover.

Yet it was an African American woman's shapely, fit body on the cover of one of the most successful diet books of 2004—Dr. David Heber's *The L.A. Shape Diet: The 14-Day Total Weight-Loss Plan*—which set out to change the "fitness perspective" for African American women. Dr. Heber's book combines the sound nutritional basis of the Color Code, building a health diet based on color fruits and vegetables, with his newest research from the UCLA Center for Human Nutrition. The book shows readers how to analyze body shape, personal protein needs, and metabolism, not only to lose weight but also to change their body shape.[8]

Dr. Heber maintains that everyone is born with a particular shape, and this shape makes a huge difference in how a person should approach weight loss. He teaches the difference between the shape a person can change and the shape a person cannot, and helps individuals find their "personal protein prescription" to best achieve their goals.

Whether in the success stories of those who completed Heber's program or in the photo of a shapely, fit African American woman on the front cover, the *L.A. Shape Diet* book uses the African American woman's body type as the symbol of an ideal body type for all women in America.

CONCLUSION

African American body types and body images, both male and female, are finally becoming a part of mainstream America, not only in the fitness, fashion, advertising, modeling, and entertainment industries, but also as preferred body types and body images for most Americans.

Another strong indication of this cultural revolution among Americans can be seen in the results of a recent survey conducted by *Fitness Magazine*. According to the magazine's 2006 poll of 1,700 Americans, 42 percent of men and 27 percent of women say that their arms are the body part they are happiest with, and 24 percent of women and 12 percent of men are happy with their backsides. Additionally, 36 percent of women and 48 percent of men say their abdominal muscles are the body part they would most like to change.

Yet the most startling finding was women's response to the question "Which of these celebrities has the most ideal body?"

The "ideal body" referred to a woman with a physically fit, well-proportioned body (breast, waist, and hip sizes) and beautiful facial features. Potential selections were Halle Berry, Jennifer Lopez, Angelina Jolie, Jennifer Aniston, Jessica Simpson, and Jennifer Garner.

Respondents selected the following:[9]

Halle Berry	25%
Jennifer Lopez	18%
Angelina Jolie	15%
Jennifer Aniston	9%
Jessica Simpson	4%
Jennifer Garner	3%

Of all the admired celebrities they could have chosen, respondents selected African American actress Halle Berry as the woman with the body type that they preferred. Apparently, she fulfills all the qualifications of an ideal body type: physically fit and well-proportioned, with beautiful facial features. Even with a margin of error of plus or minus 3.1 percentage points, this is a startling finding, which further indicates an increasing mainstream acceptance of African American body types.

Indeed, African American body types and body images are not only changing the fashion, fitness, advertising, modeling, and entertainment industries, but they are also changing body image ideals for an increasing number of Americans.

CHAPTER 2

RACE AND BODY IMAGE

INTRODUCTION

As I reflect upon my childhood years, I cannot say exactly when I began to prefer a certain body image for myself, but I can say that as early as five years old, I knew that I wanted to have a body like the world-class track and field athletes. In my African American family and neighborhood during the 1950s and 1960s, track and field athletes were greatly admired, simply because this was a sport that all the neighborhood kids could compete in and play every day. My older brothers and numerous other kids in the neighborhood naturally gravitated to the vacant lot in our neighborhood to perform our track and field events. Whether it was long jump, high jump, or sprints, all of the boys and girls in the neighborhood competed in some type of track and field event—and most importantly, we had hours of fun doing it.

This childhood experience with my four older brothers and our friends made a major impression on me, not only fostering the love of competitive sports but also showing me the type of body image that I most admired and wanted to emulate. I admired men and women who had muscular, fit-looking bodies, like Olympic competitors. Athletes like sprinter Bob Hayes and boxer Cassius Clay (aka Muhammad Ali) were the best in the world, and quite naturally I, along with many of my friends, wanted to be just like them, particularly in body type. By the age of five I knew which type of body images I most admired and wanted to emulate.

In order to have a constructive dialogue and discussion about the issues of race and body image, we must be open-minded and prepared to view these two topics from a completely different perspective than we may be used to.

No longer does our viewpoint begin from mainstream society's perspective; it actually begins from another group's—that of the African American population. Once we establish the African American perspective as our reference point for this discussion, then the majority of the assertions I will make will likely be viewed very differently and will be better understood. So take this moment to put yourself in the body and mind of an African American. What this basically means is that your world as an African American is different than the general mainstream American world because of the impact of your cultural history of slavery, segregation and second-class citizen status in the United States influences how you perceive yourself (whether negative or positive) and how others perceive you (whether negative or positive). So as an African American, you're always striving to find your self identity particularly in a society that has historically not respected you for who you are and within a community (African American) that strives to maintain its foundation and self-worth. Whether as a mature adult, a younger adult, a teenager, or a child, approach this book's issues from that point of view.

DEFINING RACE

First and foremost, the issue of race is still a highly controversial topic for most people to discuss, let alone research. Unfortunately, in our Western society, the term "race" is more often used for social and political purposes, rather than in its biological meaning. When the term "race" is more associated with its biological meaning, it does convey certain mixed messages that may be viewed as being biased toward (or against) some groups or individuals. some groups and individuals may view as very biased.

Here are some typical definitions of the word "race":

Race is defined as persons who are relatively homogeneous with respect to biological inheritance.[1]

Race is defined as a scientific, biogenetic concept, a phenotypically and/or geographically distinctive subspecific group, composed of individuals inhabiting a defined geographic and/or ecological region, and possessing characteristic phenotypic and gene frequencies that distinguish it from such groups.[2]

Human races are generally defined in terms of original geographic range and common hereditary traits which may be morphological, serological, hematological, immunological, or biochemical.[3]

As you can see, there is a great deal of variation in the definition of race in our Western society. For the sake of the discussion in this book, we will associate the term more with its social and cultural constructs, rather than its biological constructs. If we take this perspective, we can better understand certain ethnic groups' (i.e., African Americans, Latino Americans,

European Americans, Asian Americans, and American Indians) preferences for certain body images and body types.

Many researchers have argued that cultural differences are primarily responsible for ethnic groups' preferences for certain body images and body types. The results of several studies indicate that African Americans have ideals of body type and preferences in body image that are different from those of other groups.[4]

For example, a study titled "Does Ethnicity Influence Body-Size Preference? A Comparison of Body Image and Body Size" examined body-image and body-size assessments in a large sample of men and women of four ethnicities or races: black, Hispanic, Asian, and white.[5] The researchers hypothesized that black women and men would report less body dissatisfaction than the other ethnic groups; that black and Hispanic men and women, compared with Asians and whites, would accept heavier female figures and would select larger sizes as representing overweight and obese female figures (i.e., would have higher thresholds for what they consider obesity); that regardless of ethnicity, women would be more dissatisfied with their size and shape than men; and that women, compared with men, would select thinner female figures as attractive and acceptable.

From this study of 1,229 participants (801 women and 428 men, of which 288 were Asian, 548 Hispanic, 208 African American, and 185 white), the researchers found that Asian women chose a somewhat larger female figure as being underweight than did African American women. Asian women also reported less body dissatisfaction than the other groups. In terms of the interaction between gender and race, white women chose the thinnest figure as being most attractive to men, and African American men chose the heaviest.

In summary, this study investigated body image and perceptions of attractive, acceptable, and typical female figures, across a range of sizes from underweight to obese, in a large sample of Asian, African American, Hispanic, and white men and women. Wide ranges of age, educational level, and BMI were represented, and differences in these variables among groups were controlled. The findings suggested that ethnicity alone does not markedly influence perceptions of female body size. However, cultural acceptance of larger sizes may produce the tendency to be overweight in the first place. This cultural acceptance of larger sizes directly applies to the African American community.

RACE AND BODY IMAGE ISSUES IN THE MEDIA AND CELEBRITIES

In 2007, one of the most widely recognized media events related to race and body image among celebrities occurred when radio personality Don Imus described the physical features and body images of an African American women's college basketball team on his nationally televised radio talk show. Although he may not have known at the time how derogatory, demeaning, and stereotypical the words and images that he used are, Mr. Imus very shortly realized the impact of his statements.

Specifically, on April 4, 2007, Imus and his executive producer, Bernard McGuirk, discussed the NCAA women's basketball championship game between Rutgers University (a team consisting of eight African American players) and the University of Tennessee. During the discussion, Imus and McGuirk watched footage of the previous night's game.

According to transcripts from the show, here are the major comments:

Imus: That's some rough girls from Rutgers, man, they got tattoos.

McGuirk: Some hardcore hoes.

Imus: That's some nappy-headed hoes there, I'm going to tell you. (*The A&T Register* 2007: 2)

Needless to say, this conversation ignited controversy from the moment the words fell from the radio show host's lips. It took Imus two days to issue a public apology to the women of the Rutgers team for the comments that were made on his show in reference to them and other African Americans.[6]

The CBS Corporation ended the weeklong confrontation over Imus's racial and sexual insult when it canceled the *Imus in the Morning* program. The move came a day after the cable television network MSNBC (a division of General Electric that has simulcast Mr. Imus's radio program for the last ten years) removed the show from its morning lineup. These two actions, taken together, mean that Mr. Imus, who had broadcasted the program for more than thirty years, no longer has a home on either national radio or national television.[7]

After CBS chief executive Leslie Moonves met with African American community activists and representatives such as Reverend Al Sharpton and Reverend Jesse Jackson, and in light of the fact that corporate sponsors no longer wanted to support Imus's show, Mr. Moonves released the following statement:

Those who have spoken with us the last few days represent people of good will from all segments of our society—all races, economic groups, men and women alike. In our meetings with concerned groups, there has been much discussion of the [effect that] language like this has on our young people, particularly young women of color trying to make their way in this society.[8]

This statement by the chief executive of CBS, as well as the actions by the networks, indicates that mainstream media and corporations are becoming much more aware of the cultural sensitivity surrounding race and body images. That is, if people are going to discuss issues related to body images with certain racial and/or ethnic groups in the national media, they must be cognizant of the sensitive nature of this topic. If this is not taken into consideration, then what happened to Don Imus could occur again.

Another heated controversy and discussion occurred when the issue of "ideal body image" for an African American woman was questioned by a mainstream U.S. magazine. A furor erupted in the tabloid magazines when the ex-fashion model and now talk-show host Tyra Banks was photographed in a one-piece bathing suit on a beach in Sydney, Australia, after she had gained about thirty pounds. The captions that accompanied the photos in *People Magazine* said, "America's Next Top Waddle" and "Tyra Porkchop." The tabloid reports, coupled with pressure from top executives at her syndicated talk show urging her to slim down, prompted Banks to openly discuss her much-publicized weight gain:

It was such a strange meanness and rejoicing that people had when thinking that was what my body looked like. I get so much mail from young girls who say, "I look up to you; you're not as skinny as everyone else; I think you're beautiful." So when they say that my body is "ugly" and "disgusting," what does that make those girls feel like? (*People Magazine* 2007: 7)

In fact, the responses from Ms. Banks's fans were overwhelming. Here are a few of the comments about Tyra's new body:

I think she looks great either way. She is naturally curvy, and I don't mean chubby-curvy. She has hips and large breasts. I have the same problem. I will never be able to fit into a size zero, just due to my bone structure, forget about skin, fat, or muscle on top of them. I commend her for standing up and saying it's ok to be above a size 2, and you don't have the right to say those things about me. Whatever happened to the days of real Hollywood glamour and the great and curvy Marilyn Monroe body type? [Monroe] was a size ten or twelve, and no one trashes her image. That was true beauty, and Tyra fits right in with that. She encourages healthy self–images, not malnourished "model" weight goals. (Diana 1/25/07)
This is what a black woman is supposed to look like. She is the most beautiful woman in the world, and as along as she is happy, then the black men of America are happy. Only a black man can appreciate the curvaciousness of a black woman. According to a recent survey, 10 out of 10 . . . black men agree that Tyra Banks exemplifies the beauty of a real woman . . . period. (Black Men of America 1/27/07)
Tyra is beautiful. Period. End of discussion. In this country, we focus so much on weight, and we tend to judge people initially by this factor if we do not know them personally. If 161 pounds is fat for a person who is over 5' 8", then 99 percent of Americans are severely obese. There are millions of people that diet and exercise everyday to look like Tyra even after she gained 30 pounds. She is a black woman, which could mean that her genetics are responsible for curvaceous hips and thighs. Personally, I prefer to be curvy compared to being thin and "buttless." I am 5' 2", 125 pounds with lots of "rear," and I get more complements regarding my figure than most of my severely thin friends. The real question is, what is beauty? Tyra is a millionaire. Do you think she cares about how the public feels about her weight? If she did, she has more than enough

available funds to have surgery or hire a trainer without us knowing. Before we question Tyra's weight, we should reevaluate our own habits. (Ms. Naomi 1/31/07) (http://offtherack.people.com/2007/01/share_your_thou.

As a result of fans' overwhelming positive response, Ms. Banks launched a new segment on her talk show called the "So What" campaign. The "So What" campaign debuted with an episode of *The Tyra Banks Show* in which the entire audience wore the same red bathing suit that Tyra wore on the cover of *People* magazine. The purpose of this episode, and of the "So What" campaign, was to encourage women to celebrate and embrace their bodies—curves, cellulite dimples, stretch marks, and all.

The examples of Imus and Banks illustrate how important body image is to African Americans today, and shows their preference for maintaining a certain body image (both female and male)—as well as their desire for others to become more aware of the sensitive nature of African American body images.

Taking those issues into account, one of the key questions is, how do individuals learn preferred body images, and are these learned body images racially and/or ethnically based?

ENCULTURATION OF PREFERRED BODY IMAGES

In this book, we will define culture as a system of shared beliefs, values, and traditions that are transmitted from generation to generation through learning. Culture plays a vital role in shaping all of our beliefs, attitudes, and behaviors—including our preferences for certain body images. In the United States, the cultural preoccupation with weight and body shape is as strong as ever, although the new cultural trend is to attain the perfect (slim) body through exercise rather than diet.[9] Yet how do individuals within a society learn the patterns that are preferred among the members of their society? This process is referred to as *enculturation*.

Enculturation is defined as the process whereby individuals learn the behavioral standards of a particular cultural trait within their society or group. Enculturation is a process, because usually individuals go through a series of steps (success and failures) that determine whether they meet with the approval or acceptance of that cultural trait in a particular group (i.e., ethnic, social, educational, gender, or age groups).

One of the best ways to see how enculturation really works is to examine its attributes. The major attributes of enculturation are:

1. It's a learned process
2. It's transmitted by symbols
3. It adds meaning to reality
4. It's differently shared

5. It's integrated
6. It's adaptive.[10]

Enculturation relates directly to our preferred body images, because all of us learn a preferred body image for women, men, boys, and girls that is highly influenced by immediate family members, extended family members, friends, social groups, and ethnic groups, as well as mainstream society's groupings.

Enculturation is transmitted by symbols, both verbal and nonverbal. In the diet and fitness field, U.S. society tends to show a preference for certain body types (thin to slim) in magazines, television, advertisements, and the entertainment world that are perceived as healthy—whereas those who do not fit this category (those who are full-figured or shapely) are not perceived as healthy. Symbolically, the approved body types (thin to slim) become the norm in society and do not allow for much variation.[11]

Enculturation adds meaning to reality. For example, children, adolescents, and adults participate in beauty contests to find out whether they are the most "beautiful" in their age category. If a certain individual, with a certain body type, is selected as the winner of a beauty contest, then it is not only her personality but also her body type being selected as representing society's beauty standards.

Enculturation is differently shared. In general, African Americans view body image differently than European Americans, for instance. Not only is there variation between African Americans and European Americans, but there is also much variation in beliefs about body image within the African American population.

Enculturation is integrated. In other words, body image must be viewed as integrated in the totality of one's life, because it may be directly related to the individual's income (whether he or she can afford to join a fitness program), geographic location (whether he or she lives in an area that promotes certain body images and body types—for instance, thinner on the west coast, heavier in the southeast), and historical issues (whether he or she has had a history, family or individual, of acknowledging the importance of certain body images and body types).

Finally, enculturation is adaptive. In order for more of the general public to accept certain body images and body types, the public needs to have more opportunities to see a variety of body images and body types being promoted in a wide variety of activities. If this adaptive strategy were incorporated on a regular basis, then we would be better able to see and appreciate how African American body types and body images are changing the fashion, fitness, and sports apparel industries.

To better illustrate how some ethnic groups in the United States have enculturated certain types of preferred body images, I will present a review of the latest studies and data. This brief review for each ethnic group will help us to understand the impact of cultural beliefs and patterns upon our preferences for certain body images.

In order to perform this review of body images among ethnic groups, I have used the categories of ethnicity in the United States defined in Directive 15 of the U.S. Office of Management and Budget (OMB), which established standards for the collection of data on race and ethnicity. The original version of OMB Directive 15 was released in 1977; the second version was issued in 1997. The goal of the directive is

to provide consistent and comparable data on race and ethnicity throughout the federal government for an array of statistical and administrative programs. Development of the data standards stems in large measure from new responsibilities to enforce civil rights laws. Data were needed to monitor equal access to housing, education, and employment opportunities for population groups that historically had experienced discrimination and different treatment because of their race or ethnicity.[12]

Here are the categories of race according to version two of OMB Directive 15:

1. American Indian or Alaska Native—a person having origins in any of the original peoples of North America, and who maintains cultural identifications, tribal affiliation, or community recognition.
2. Asian—a person having origins in any of the original peoples of the Far East, Southeast Asia, or the Indian subcontinent, including, for example, Cambodia, China, India, Japan, Korea, Malaysia, Pakistan, the Philippine Islands, Thailand, and Vietnam.
3. Native Hawaiian or other Pacific Islander—a person having origins in any of the original peoples of Hawaii, Guam, Samoa, or the other Pacific Islands.
4. Black—a person having origins in any of the black racial groups of Africa.
5. Hispanic/Latino—a person having origins in any of the original peoples of Mexico, Puerto Rico, Cuba, Central and South America, and other Spanish-speaking countries.
6. White—a person having origins in any of the original peoples of Europe, North Africa, or the Middle East. (http://wonder.cdc.gov/wonder/help/populations/bridged-race/Directive15.html)[13]

EUROPEAN AMERICAN ENCULTURATION OF PREFERRED BODY IMAGES

Research indicates that preferred body images vary among cultures, as well as within cultures across groups and time. Within Western industrialized cultures, there have been many changes over the years in the body shape and size that is considered attractive and healthy, especially for women.[14]

Preferred Female Body Images

Historically in Western industrialized cultures, plumpness was considered fashionable and erotic. From the Middle Ages, artists idealized the "reproductive figure." The fullness of the stomach was emphasized as a symbol of fertility.[15] The female body was frequently represented with full, rounded hips and breasts. This trend is represented in popular paintings of the 1600s, which portrayed a woman with a plump body—the preferred body type of the time.[16]

The idealization of slimness in women is a very recent phenomenon, dating from the 1920s. Many scholars contend that the thin ideal is the result of successful marketing by the fashion industry, which has become the standard of cultural beauty in the affluent industrialized societies of the twentieth century.[17] Fashions in clothing were represented by hand-drawn illustrations until the 1920s, when they started to be photographed and widely distributed in mass-market fashion magazines. These magazines presented a fantasy image of how women should look. The fashions themselves demanded a molding of the female body because each "look" suited a particular body shape.[18]

In the 1930s and 1940s, ideals of beauty moved toward a shapelier figure. For instance, the mean measurements of Miss America pageant winners went from 30-25-32 in the early 1920s to 35–25–36 in the 1940s. Famous actresses such as Lana Turner and Jane Russell typified the change of preferred body images and types during this period.[19]

Although this trend of shapelier women in America, particularly in the fashion industry, continued in the 1950s (e.g., Marilyn Monroe), there was also a significant move toward slimness. Actresses such as Grace Kelly and Audrey Hepburn became role models for some young women, and slimness became associated with the upper classes.[20] This trend toward slimness became particularly acute in the 1960s, when the fashion model Twiggy became the role mode for a generation of young women. Twiggy's body type was described as a "flat-chested, boyish figure, and [she] weighed 96 lbs."[21]

Slimness came to exemplify unconventionality, freedom, youthfulness, and the "jet set" lifestyle. This trend occurred across Europe and the United States and became the foundation of the fashion industry and major media's preferences in female body types. Therefore, thin and thinner became the standard of beauty for many women from the 1960s to today. In fact, as of 2007 in the fashion industry, extreme thinness is the preferred body type for female models.[22]

Explanations for this preference for thin body images include a desire to emulate the upper class and the fashion industry, where thinness is equated with wealth, leisure, and fame; women's roles changing from maternal to more instrumental or masculine venues and occupations; a desire to appear youthful; and a perceived association between thinness and health, as promoted by the medical community. The potential negative consequences of the thin ideal include negative body image, low self-esteem, and psychological and physical disorders of life-threatening proportions.[23]

Preferred Male Body Images

Western representations of the male body also have an interesting history. Contemporary Western cultures derive much of their preferences in male body images from ancient Greece and Rome. Sculptors in ancient Greece were keenly interested in the problems of realistically representing the human figure, and it was at this stage in history that lifelike male nudes started to appear. Men were often presented nude, whereas women were represented clothed in cloaks and undergarments. The male body was revered and considered more attractive than the female body.[24]

In the seventh century BCE, there emerged a trend for a broad-shouldered, narrow-hipped ideal that has become known as the Daedalic style, after the mythical Daedalus of Crete, who was, according to legend, the first Greek sculptor. At this stage, the male body was idealized and presented in a strictly stylized way, with emphasis on clearly defined muscles that were carved into the surface of the marble.[25]

Contemporary Western cultures also idealized classic Roman male figures that were depicted as slender and muscular in paintings and sculptures. The male body continued to dominate art until the mid-1800s.

By the end of the nineteenth century, the impact of sports culture had transformed the Western perspective on male bodies. The celebration of youthfulness and exuberance directed the analytical schema of advertisers that equated physical activity, especially those associated with sports, and its affects on the male body as the ideal to strive for.[26]

In 1921, when Charles Atlas (aka Angelo Siciliano) won the "World's Most Beautiful Man Contest," it helped solidify the connection between the body and physical fitness. In the following year, Atlas was declared "America's Most Perfectly Developed Man." The Charles Atlas body was described as muscular, smooth, and well-proportioned, evoking perfect manhood and confidence. It is interesting that what Charles Atlas sold was less about his body and more about the image of confidence in one's physical self—an ebullient "body love" in which the body seemed less important than the freedom to love it.[27]

Although the Charles Atlas body became the preferred image for several decades, it was not until the 1980s that idealized images of the naked (or semi-naked) male body became common in mainstream Western media.

Muscular actors such as Arnold Schwarzenegger, Jean-Claude Van Damme, and Dolph Lundgren exemplified the well-muscled male ideal.[28]

Presently, the preferred male body type is slender and moderately muscular. Clearly, the social pressure on men is different and less extreme than on women, as men still tend to be judged in terms of achievements rather than looks. However, there is a growing interest in men's body shape and size. European American men are under increased social pressure to conform to the muscular, well-toned, mesomorphic (medium-sized) shape, and most scholars expect this cultural shift to continue for decades.

HISPANIC/LATINO ENCULTURATION TO PREFERRED BODY IMAGES

Although there have been numerous studies investigating mainstream European American cultures' preferences for certain body types and images, very little historical and contemporary studies have focused on the preferences of other ethnic populations such as the Hispanics/Latinos. According to the U.S. Census Bureau, in 1980 there were approximately 14.6 million Hispanics/Latinos living in the United States. By 2000 that number had dramatically increased by nearly 142 percent to 35.3 million. Currently, the Hispanic/Latino population is the largest ethnic minority group in the United States.[29]

The umbrella term *Hispanic* is used to conveniently describe a large and diverse population. A person with a Hispanic/Latino background is one whose conditions and events surrounding and influencing his or her life, including education, language, experiences, and health beliefs, are associated with Spanish civilization.[30] Each Hispanic group, however, is distinct and unique, with its own history. Each group has its own relation to this country, and each tends to be concentrated in different geographic areas.[31]

The Hispanic/Latino population in the United States is divided into five main subgroups: Mexican Americans, Puerto Ricans, Cuban Americans, Central and South Americans, and people of other Hispanic origins. Mexican Americans are the largest subgroup, comprising nearly 60 percent of the Hispanic/Latino population, and Puerto Ricans are the second largest. Together, they account for over two-thirds of the Hispanic/Latino population.[32]

Interestingly, the majority of the body-image studies regarding the Hispanic/Latino population have been comparative studies conducted alongside European Americans.[33] Although evidence from these studies suggests that the body image of Hispanics/Latinos do not differ from European Americans, one study contradicted this finding.

Altabe (1998),[34] in particular, found that Hispanic/Latino adults had a more positive body image as indicated by higher self-ratings of attractiveness in comparison to European Americans. In that qualitative analysis of ideal traits, Altabe found that both Hispanic/Latino and European American college students (men and women) valued being tall and tan. The European Americans idealized blond hair, whereas Hispanic/Latinos idealized brown hair and brown eyes. Thus the typical Hispanic/Latino physical traits (brown hair and eyes, darker skin) were viewed positively by this sample.[35]

Overall, issues of general appearance and ideal Hispanic/Latino physical traits have not been investigated in-depth. Because the majority of the studies on Hispanic/Latino culture have been comparative studies, more culture-specific studies need to be conducted in order to discover the diversity of ideals regarding body images. The ideal of thinness in Hispanic/Latino culture is relatively new and may not be the representative preference of the entire group. Therefore, future studies need to examine Hispanics/Latinos within their more heterogeneous cultural groups, which include Mexican, Puerto Rican, Cuban, Central American, South American, or other Spanish culture of origin, as some subtle and unique cultural characteristics may be overlooked when they are considered a single homogenous ethnic group.[36]

ASIAN AND PACIFIC ISLANDER ENCULTURATION TO PREFERRED BODY IMAGES

Another population that has received very little attention regarding their opinions and beliefs on preferred body images are Asian and Pacific Islanders. Asian Americans are defined as the federally designated ethnic populations whose origins are in Asia. Individuals of Asian descent who are U.S. citizens or permanent residents of the country are considered Asian Americans. According to census designations, Asian Americans include, but are not limited to, those who self-classify as Asian Indians, Cambodians, Chinese, Filipino, Hmong, Japanese, Korean, Laotian, Thai, Vietnamese, and "other."[37]

Pacific Islanders are defined as individuals who are descendants of the original residents of the Pacific Islands under the jurisdiction of the U.S. government. According to census designation, Pacific Islanders include, but are not limited to, Chamorro, Hawaiians, Melanesians, Micronesians, Polynesians, Samoans, and "other" Pacific Islanders.[38]

In general, over thirty different ethnic subgroups make up the Asian and Pacific Islander populations, with each subgroup having its distinctive cultural traditions, languages, and values. There is a great deal of intra-group and inter-group variability among members of the Asian and Pacific Islander population in terms of the degree of acculturation, generation, and immigration experiences. Despite this variability, similarities in terms of traditional cultural values, status as an ethnic minority group, and in particular physical appearance (which may differ from Western notions of beauty) also exist.[39]

For example, recent studies among Pacific Islanders (adults identified as Native Hawaiians, Samoans, Tongans, Cook Islanders, and Maori) showed that they preferred a larger body size than European Americans.[40] In addition, one study showed that Pacific Islanders with a higher body mass index

(BMI) were more likely to see themselves as "underweight" or the "right weight" in comparison to European Americans.[41] These findings are consistent with traditional views among Pacific Islanders that place great importance on larger body size as this represents high status, power, authority, and wealth.[42]

Some Asian cultures, such as those in Korea, China, Japan, and the Philippines, have traditionally viewed obesity as a sign of prosperity, good health, or beauty. Current research and observations indicate that this is no longer the case among young women in modern industrialized Asia.[43]

Currently, comparative studies with European Americans have provided inconsistent findings. For example, an analysis of twenty-two studies on body image or other related behaviors in Asians and European Americans found three sets of findings:

1. Asians showed more concerns than European Americans about their body image.
2. Asians showed no differences with European Americans about their body image.
3. Asian males had less concerns than European American males about their body image.[44]

Yet one major factor that may mediate and/or moderate body image concerns and change strategies among Asian cultural groups is that, unlike in Western culture, some cultures, such as the Chinese, do not place as much importance on male muscularity.[45]

Recently, a research team conducted a two-study research on male body images in Taiwan and Western society. Specifically, the team hypothesized that Taiwanese men would exhibit less dissatisfaction with their bodies than their Western counterparts, and that Taiwanese advertising would place less value on the male body than Western media.[46]

For the first study, fifty-five Taiwanese male undergraduate students at a university in Taiwan were recruited. The self-identified heterosexual male students participated in this study "examining body image perception," in which their height, weight, and body fat would be measured, followed by a brief computerized test. The results from this phase of the study were then compared with previous results of men from the United States and Europe. The researchers found men in both the East and the West preferred to be more muscular. But when the study participants were asked to identify what male body type women preferred, the Taiwanese men appeared much more comfortable with their body image than their Western counterparts. Further investigation found that American men believed that American women preferred a male body with about 20 pounds more muscle than an average American man, whereas Taiwanese men estimated only a 5 pound difference.[47]

For the second study, the research team compared the value of the male body in American versus Taiwanese magazine advertising, using their method of counting dressed and undressed models in women's magazines. For the United States, they chose the two leading women's magazines, *Cosmopolitan* and *Glamour*. For Taiwan, they chose the comparable *Bella* and *Vivi*, as well as the Taiwanese version of *Cosmopolitan*.

In the Taiwanese magazines from 2001, the research team found more than 1,000 advertisements that used male or female models, advertising a wide variety of products—some body-related (e.g., clothes, perfume) and others not (e.g., food, tobacco)—from both Western and Asian manufacturers. When they compared the Taiwanese advertisements with their earlier American data, they found only modest differences in the prevalence of undressed models of both sexes, even though the Taiwanese magazines actually showed more nudity. Asian women, however, were portrayed undressed only about half as often as Western women in the Taiwanese magazines, and most striking, Asian men were almost never shown undressed. Of the seventy-eight Asian men in the Taiwanese magazine advertisements, only four (5%) were shown undressed, compared to 43 percent of Western men and 43 percent of Western women in the same magazines.[48]

The researchers concluded from their two studies (*Body Image in Taiwanese Men* and *Male Body Image in Taiwanese and American Magazine Advertising*) that American culture, and perhaps other Western cultures, have become much more focused on male body appearance than Chinese culture (they use the term *Chinese culture* because 98 percent of the Taiwanese population are of Chinese origin, with the majority of their traditional cultural values derived almost exclusively from Chinese traditions). What accounts for this difference?

They propose three hypotheses:

1. Chinese culture places less emphasis on muscularity as a measure of masculinity.
2. Chinese men are less exposed to muscular images common in American media.
3. Chinese men have experienced less change in their traditional roles as "head of the household" than men in the United States and other Western countries.[49]

Overall, the differences in preferred body images among Asians and Pacific Islanders have been found to be the result of an increase in, or lack of, exposure to Western cultures. Though younger Asian and Asian American women are probably aware of traditional Asian ideals that promote weight gain, they seem to be more likely to subscribe to Western ideals of thinness. Moreover, as in Western cultures, there appears to be less of an emphasis on physical appearance for men, and therefore less is known about the ideal body image of Asian and Asian American men. Additional research, particularly qualitative research, that asks Asian American and Pacific Islander women and men what they perceive to be the traditional ideals of beauty would elucidate the difference between traditional and Western notions of beauty.[50]

NATIVE AMERICAN AND ALASKA NATIVES ENCULTURATION TO PREFERRED BODY IMAGES

Not surprisingly, another population that has received very little attention and research regarding their opinions and beliefs about preferred body images are the Native American and Alaska Native populations. Of the few studies conducted on body image in these populations, Native Americans displayed more concern with their body image than European Americans.[51]

One of the main variables that may affect the differences observed between Native Americans and European Americans is BMI. Where assessed, Native Americans had a higher BMI, and they were more likely to perceive themselves as overweight in comparison to European Americans.[52] However, the higher levels of concern with body image and symptoms of eating disorders found among First Nations may also be indicative of the feelings of displacement and alienation in urban areas, a loss of their ethnic identity, and a non-supportive community.[53] As with other ethnic minorities, an important factor to further examine is the individual's identification with his or her own cultural group.[54]

CONCLUSION

After reading the various sections on each ethnic group's preferences toward certain body images and body types, it should be apparent that there is still much variation between and within populations. Interestingly, most studies in this regard use a comparative method—that is, researchers continue to compare specific ethnic populations with the European American population. Yet these studies fall substantially short in finding out the true underlying *cultural reasons* for the differing body image and body type preferences between the ethnic and the European American populations.

In order to obtain a deeper understanding and appreciation of the various racial and ethnic variations in this preference, particularly in the African American population, we must conduct substantially more studies *within* a specific ethnic population and move away from the approach that compares it to European Americans. We must also incorporate more qualitative studies that will reveal rich, sensitive, and culturally competent data on preferred body images and body types. This is one of the main objectives of this book.

—— CHAPTER 3 ——

BODY IMAGE PREFERENCES AMONG AFRICAN AMERICANS

INTRODUCTION

After publishing *Food Choice and Obesity in Black America: Creating a New Cultural Diet* and promoting my book at signings and presentations for more than a year, an interesting phenomenon occurred on the tour. The African Americans who attended often shared stories with me and the audience about the importance to them of "body image." In fact, they were quite descriptive about the types of bodies (male and female) they preferred. Interestingly, all African Americans in the audience replied in the affirmative when asked whether African Americans preferred a particular body type.

In addition to the very positive comments about preferred body types among African Americans present at my talks, another interesting trend developed during this period. It involved the Web site I developed, www.newblackculturaldiet.com, to continue the dialogue about the importance of health, physical fitness, dieting, and body image among African Americans and those who share similar lifestyles.

One method of sharing information with visitors to the Web site has been through the production of podcast shows. Podcast shows—or podcasting—is a new way for individuals to communicate what they are passionate about or want to talk about with others. Basically, a podcast show is an audio recording of one's voice and/or music on an mp3 file on the computer that any individual can upload to his or her Web site, and which visitors can download and listen to. Podcasting is an effective method for reaching hundreds of thousands of listeners, using minimum equipment and resources.[1]

Interestingly, during this year-long period of promoting my book, I recorded more than ten podcast shows. The podcasts covered topics such as food selection and preparation, exercise and physical fitness, African American men's preventive health practices, African American women's preventive health practices, African American kids' preventive health practices, and—especially—the subject of body image. Our podcast on body image was the first show produced, and it immediately became the most consistently downloaded podcast for the entire year (2006–2007).

The major topics that my co-host and I discussed during this podcast, which focused entirely on African American body image, included these:

• The preferred body types among African American women and men
• The natural curves of an African American woman as a positive physical attribute
• The natural muscular features of an African American male as a desired physical attribute
• The double standard in the African American community about preferred body images. This double standard involves the concept of a body that looks "too African American" or "too European American," and causes some people to feel uncomfortable about their own ethnic physical identity (natural curves, hips, rear end) or to think that another person is losing his or her ethnic physical identity (curves, hips, rear end).

Not only did this podcast remain the number one downloaded show for the entire year, but it signified that this topic—body image—was an important and intriguing issue to visitors to the Web site.

OUR VIEWS ON BODY IMAGE

Think about how often you have heard or used the following phrases:

That boy needs some meat on his bones!
There's nothing wrong with him; he's just very "healthy."
I like my women "thick," with some hips on them.
Why are you exercising; you're going to be too thin!"
There's just more of me to love.
There must be somethin' wrong with him/her—he/she looks like he/she lost some weight!

These comments, and so many more, reflect the African American perspective that for one to be healthy, he or she must be at least well proportioned (with noticeable hips, stomach, thighs, and breasts)—even bordering on overweight—and must definitely not be too thin (perceived as an indication of having contracted HIV/AIDS or of having an eating disorder). Moreover, these comments reflect the African American "flexible cultural definition of healthiness." This definition means, in other words, that it is good in the African American community to have some "meat on your bones," primarily because having such a body type indicates that one has more than enough food to eat and enough income and leisure time in which to consume the ample food.

On one hand, the "flexible cultural definition of healthiness" can actually be to the advantage of African Americans because it allows for varying degrees of acceptable body types within the culture, preventing a narrow definition of which body type constitutes the healthy one. On the other hand, the flexibility promotes acceptance of overweight and obesity as the norm within the African American community. As the more accepted and more ideal body type in the African American population becomes the heavier one, as opposed to the thinner one, tremendous medical and quality-of-life concerns (e.g., hypertension, diabetes, and cardiovascular disease) arise.

Nonetheless, the African American flexible cultural definition of healthiness is one that mainstream society actually wishes that it could truly embrace and incorporate into its culture and values pattern, for the preference for thinness within mainstream U.S. society has contributed to eating disorders such as anorexia and bulimia among white males and females. In addition to bearing the imprint of the cultural pattern of thinness, U.S. mainstream society receives constant messages and pressure through the media and at the workplace, and from the entertainment, fitness, and fashion industries to stay or to become thin.[2]

RESEARCH ON AFRICAN AMERICAN BODY IMAGE, BODY SIZE, AND BODY TYPE PREFERENCES

To provide a better understanding of African American body image, body size, and body-type preferences, this chapter highlights several recent studies that examine the subject in the African American and other U.S. populations. This section is divided into four age- and school-based groupings: (1) elementary school, (2) middle and high School, (3) college, and (4) professional adults. The grouping of African Americans into age- and school-based categories will provide a better understanding of the variation and diversity of opinions within the African American population with regard to body image, body size, and body-type preferences.[3]

Body Image in Elementary School

A study conducted in thirteen northern California public elementary schools, titled "Overweight Concerns and Body Dissatisfaction among Third-Grade Children: The Impacts of Ethnicity and Socioeconomic Status," examined the prevalence of body image concerns and body dissatisfaction among third-grade girls and boys, as influenced by ethnicity and socioeconomic status (SES). This study assessed overweight concerns; body dissatisfaction;

and desired shape, height, and weight among 969 children (mean age, 8.5 years).[4]

Of the 999 third-grade children enrolled in the thirteen schools, 969 (97.0 percent) participated in the study. Parents refused participation for 29 children, and 1 child was absent during the study. By ethnic breakdown, participants in the study were 44 percent white, 21 percent Latino, 19 percent Asian American (not including Filipino), 8 percent Filipino, 5 percent African American, 1 percent American Indian, and 1 percent Pacific Islander. Slightly more than 50 percent of the participants (50.2 percent) were girls, and boys in the sample were slightly older (8.5 years vs. 8.4 years) than girls. The researchers drew their data from responses to the Kids' Eating Disorders Survey (KEDS).[5]

As hypothesized, the research team found that girls reported greater concern about overweight and greater body dissatisfaction, and desired thinner body shapes than boys. After accounting for sex differences, ethnic differences were assessed separately for boys and girls. Among girls, African Americans had significantly more overweight concerns than Asian Americans and Filipinos; and Latinas had significantly more overweight concerns than whites, Asian Americans, and Filipinas. White and Latina girls reported greater body dissatisfaction than Asian American girls.[6]

To examine whether ethnic differences could be explained by differences in actual body fatness, comparisons were repeated after stratifying the girls into three body mass index (BMI) groups: (1) girls with a BMI *at or below* the 25th percentile for the entire sample; (2) girls with a BMI between the 25th and 75th percentile; and (3) girls with a BMI at or above the 75th percentile. Data indicated that overweight concerns and body dissatisfaction increased with increasing BMI in all ethnic groups.

After groups were stratified by BMI, significant ethnic differences in overweight concerns persisted only in the large middle stratum. Among these girls, Latinas reported significantly more overweight concerns than whites and Asian Americans, and there was a trend toward greater overweight concerns among African Americans compared with whites (p = 0.05). There were no significant differences in body dissatisfaction or desired body shape among girls or among boys.[7]

Overall, this study indicates that African American and Hispanic girls are not immune to cultural emphasis on extreme thinness. Latina and African American third-grade girls reported greater or equivalent levels of dysfunctional eating attitudes and behaviors in comparison with white girls, even after controlling for actual body fatness and SES. The findings suggest that body dissatisfaction and body image concerns are prevalent across sex, ethnicity, and socioeconomic class. They also indicate a need for culturally appropriate school-based primary prevention programs designed specifically for Latino and African American children.[8]

In their study "Ideal Body Size Beliefs and Weight Concerns of Fourth-Grade Children," Thompson, Corwin, and Sargent explored whether preferences for body image, size, and type are formulated earlier than the junior high or high school years. This study assessed racial and gender differences in perceptions of ideal body size among white and African American fourth-grade children.[9]

The researchers surveyed a random sample of fourth-graders at small, medium, and large South Carolina elementary schools. The final sample of participants consisted of 817 fourth-graders aged eight to twelve years (mean age = 9.3 years). Demographically, the sample comprised 51.8 percent white children and 48.2 percent African American children, of whom 51.4 percent were girls and 48.6 percent were boys. The survey collected information in the following areas: demographics, dieting and weight concern, body image, and body size perception.

When students were asked to select a picture that "looks most like you," the researchers found that among these fourth-graders, African American males selected a larger self than white males. Additionally, African American females selected a significantly heavier self than white females. As for selecting an ideal female and male child size, African American females selected a larger female child than did white females.[10]

Overall, this study indicates that even at this point in the sociocultural development of children, the factors of gender, SES, and ethnicity are of great influence in selecting ideal body size and in determining body size satisfaction. African American children selected significantly heavier ideal sizes than did white children for self, male child, adult male, and adult female.[11]

Similarly, in their study titled "Discrepancies in Body Image Perception among Fourth-Grade Public School Children from Urban, Suburban, and Rural Maryland," Welch et al. found that African American elementary children chose larger figures than did whites and children of other races to represent their current and ideal images, and the African American children were most satisfied with their body size. The objective of this study was to determine whether there is an association between body image perception and weight status as measured by the BMI among a group of fourth-graders in Maryland.[12]

The sample consisted of 524 fourth-grade public school students (54 percent girls, 46 percent boys) from three geographically distinct regions in Maryland (38.6 percent urban, 30.7 percent suburban, 30.7 percent rural). Of the total sample, 60.7 percent (318 students) were white, 30.9 percent (162 students) were African American, 3.4 percent (18 students) were Hispanic, 2.1 percent (11 students) were Asian or Pacific Islander, and 2.9 percent (15 students) were of some other ethnic background. Approximately 39 percent of the students were from an urban setting, and the other two geographic locations were equally represented (30.7 percent of students were from suburban Maryland; 30.7 percent were from rural Maryland).[13]

The researchers used silhouettes of children to test their sample's body image perception. The pictorials consisted of images of girls and boys, numbered 1 to 7, to correspond with increases in size from very thin to obese. The fourth-graders were asked to select images that most looked like them (current body image) and that looked the way they wanted to look (ideal body image). A body image discrepancy score was calculated by subtracting the number of the silhouettes chosen as having the ideal body image from the number of the silhouettes chosen as reflecting the students' current body image. These scores were then sorted into three categories: (1) Participant desires to be thinner (discrepancy scores greater than zero); (2) Participant is satisfied with current image (discrepancy scores equal to zero); and (3) Participant desires to be bigger (discrepancy scores less than zero).

The researchers found that current body image scores did not differ significantly for boys and girls. However, boys had a significantly larger ideal image than girls. Approximately 47 percent of the fourth-graders were satisfied with their current image, while the others wanted to be either smaller (42 percent) or larger (11 percent). Urban children had a higher ideal image than their suburban and rural counterparts. Additionally, more children from rural areas (47.2 percent) wanted to lose weight than did children from urban areas (38.6 percent).[14]

Most important, the study found that African American students had significantly higher current image and ideal image scores than did white students and students of other race or ethnicity. In other words, African American fourth-graders selected significantly larger figures to represent their current and ideal images than did white, Hispanic, Asian/Pacific Islander, and other students.[15]

Overall, the research team suggests that their study highlights the fact that body image preferences are formed early in life. Caregivers, educators, and health professionals therefore must be mindful of the messages they send young children. Dietitians in particular, by using culturally appropriate materials, can educate both young people and adults about healthy weight, nutrition, exercise, and body image.[16]

Body Image in Middle and High School

In "Body Image and Weight Concerns among African American and White Adolescent Females: Differences that Make a Difference," Parker et al. examined body image and dieting behaviors among African American and white adolescent females.[17] They explored specifically the cultural factors that have an impact on weight perception, body image, beauty, and style.

In this study, 250 eighth grade (junior high) and ninth grade (senior high school) girls were recruited. Informants were 75 percent white, 16 percent Mexican American, and 9 percent Asian American. In the final year of the project, a second sample of forty-six African American adolescent girls, drawn from grades nine through twelve and from various community groups in the same city, was added to the study. The researchers' study of African American adolescent girls utilized both ethnographic interview and survey methods. Ten focus group discussions with four to five girls per group were conducted by African American researchers in order to identify the perceptions and concerns of African American girls regarding their weight and body image, dieting, and other, broader health and lifestyle matters.[18]

The research team consisted of both white and African American researchers. Focus group and individual interviews were transcribed, read, and discussed by members of the research team. Cultural differences and similarities that emerged from the data were analyzed in weekly meetings among the researchers. Later, a panel of community members was asked to comment on the findings.[19]

The researchers stated that what was particularly striking in African American girls' descriptions, when compared with those of white adolescents, was the de-emphasis on external beauty as a prerequisite for popularity. As one girl noted:

There's a difference between being just fine or being just pretty . . . because I know a lot of girls who aren't just drop-dead fine but they are pretty, and they're funny, all those things come in and that makes the person beautiful There are a lot of bad-looking [physically beautiful] girls out there, but you can't stand being around them.[20]

The researchers also stated that girls were aware that African American boys had more specific physical criteria for the "ideal girl" than what they had themselves. They commented that boys like girls who are shapely, "thick," and who have "nice thighs." One girl noted that "girls would be talkin' about the butt . . . it be big."[21]

Another girl explained the following:

I think pretty matters more to guys than to me. I don't care. Just real easy to talk to, that would be the ideal girl for me, but the ideal girl from the guy's perspective would be entirely different. They want them to be fine, you know what guys like, shapely. Black guys like black girls who are thick—full figured.[22]

As for the issue of beauty, the researchers found that it was not described in relation to a particular size or set of body statistics. Girls noted that beauty was not merely a question of shape. It was more to be beautiful on the inside as well as on the outside, and to be beautiful a girl had to "know her culture." One girl explained that "African American girls have an inner beauty that they carry within them—their sense of pride."[23] This sense of pride was commonly described as a legacy they received from their mothers.[24]

Overall, the researchers stated that from their study, the standards for body image and beauty among these African American adolescents could be summed up in what these girls term "looking good." "Looking good"—or "got it goin' on"—expresses the ability of the girl to make whatever it is that she has work for her by creating and presenting a sense of style.[25]

Body Image in College

A study conducted by M. Altabe surveyed 150 male and 185 female college students attending the University of South Florida. Participants completed four different body image questionnaires and several self-ratings that included physical attractiveness and physical appearance scored on a scale of 1 to 11.[26]

Qualitative results from the sampled African Americans, Asian Americans, Caucasian Americans, and Hispanic Americans revealed that height was valued by all groups. Females in all the groups and the Asian and Caucasian males wanted to be thinner. Males in all the groups and the African American and Caucasian females wanted to be more toned. Non-Caucasian females wanted longer hair. All groups valued dark skin or wanted darker skin, except for African American females and Asian males.[27]

For general appearance body image, African Americans had the most positive self-view. Asian Americans placed the least importance on physical appearance. Thus ethnic differences occurred for both the weight and nonweight dimensions of body image.[28]

Another study on the body image of college-age subjects, titled "Comparison of Body Image Dimensions by Race/Ethnicity and Gender in a University Population," had three major objectives: (1) to examine the interaction of gender and race or ethnicity on body image dimensions, including three racial or ethnic groups in the sample; (2) to more comprehensively measure body image by assessing feelings about body parts significant to race or ethnicity; (3) to measure and control for numerous important possible factors including age, body size, SES, and social desirability.[29]

Participants were 120 college students from a northeastern (n = 27) and a southwestern (n = 93) university. The sample comprised twenty male and twenty female students in each of the three racial or ethnic groups (African American, European American, and Latino American). At the northeastern university, students were recruited from fourteen graduate or undergraduate classes in nine departments, with the permission of the instructors. At the southwestern university, participants were solicited through the research pool (primarily undergraduates) of the Department of Psychology, and were given class credit for their participation.[30]

The researchers found that African Americans scored significantly higher than European Americans and Latino Americans on the dimensions of appearance Evaluation and Body Areas Satisfaction, and scored above European Americans on the Body Esteem Scale (BES). On the other appearance dimensions, African American women rated themselves significantly higher on Sexual Attractiveness than did European American women, and Latinas scored in the middle. African American women also scored higher than other women on BES dimension of Weight Concern, showing a higher sense of self-esteem regarding their weight. The men did not differ by racial/ethnic group on the BES.[31]

Overall, the researchers suggest that their study helps to expand the database on differences and similarities in body image, based on gender and race or ethnicity. The study makes evident the need to expand the variables under consideration and to place them within a relevant cultural context in an understanding of identity, self-esteem, and self-care.[32]

Body Image among Professional Adults

A study titled "Does Ethnicity Influence Body Size Preference? A Comparison of Body Image and Body Size" examined body image and body size assessments in a large sample of men and women of four ethnic groups (Hispanic, African American, Asian, and white). The researchers hypothesized that African American women and men would report less body dissatisfaction than the other ethnic groups; that African American and Hispanic men and women, compared with Asians and whites, would accept heavier female figures and would select larger sizes as representing overweight and obesity in females (i.e., would have higher thresholds for what they consider obesity); that regardless of ethnicity, women would be more dissatisfied with their size and shape than men; and that women, compared with men, would select thinner female figures as attractive and acceptable.[33]

From this study of 1,229 participants (801 women and 428 men), of which 288 were Asian, 548 were Hispanic, 208 were African American, and 185 were white, the researchers found that Asian women chose a somewhat larger female figure as being underweight than did African American women; and that Asian women reported less body dissatisfaction than the other groups. In terms of the interaction between gender and race, white women chose the thinnest and African American men chose the heaviest female figure as attractive to men.[34]

In summary, this study investigated body image and the perception of attractive, acceptable, and typical female figures, across a range of sizes from underweight to obese, in a large community sample of Asian, African American, Hispanic, and white men and women. Wide ranges of age, educational level, and BMI were represented, and differences in these variables among groups were controlled. The findings suggested that ethnicity alone does not markedly influence perceptions of female body size. However, cultural acceptance of larger sizes may produce the initial tendency to be overweight.[35] This cultural acceptance of larger sizes directly applies to the African American community.

Another study, "Body Image Preferences among Urban African Americans and Whites from Low-Income Communities," was conducted to answer two main questions: (1) How do African American and white men and women from similar low-income communities perceive their body mass relative to others in the population? (2) Do ethnic and gender differences exist in the selection of ideal body image sizes for the same and for the opposite sex? Overall, the researchers designed this research as a community study to determine ethnic differences in the relative accuracy of self-estimates of body image and preferences for ideal body image in African American and white low-income communities.[36]

This study was conducted in East Baltimore, Maryland, where adjacent urban African American and white communities of similar low socioeconomic status reside. Nine hundred twenty-seven persons were interviewed during eight weeks and were asked to provide their height and weight and to select body size images from a standardized ethnic group-specific Figure Rating Scale that represented their current self, their ideal self, and their estimation of ideals for the opposite sex. The sample consisted of 579 African Americans (47 percent male, 53 percent female) and 348 whites (46 percent male, 54 percent female).

The researchers found that the average ideal body image for self was the same for African American men and white men, whereas African American women had a significantly greater ideal image compared with white women. Interestingly, the ideal body image for white women was most distant from the image they selected for their current self. Slightly more than one-fourth of white women were satisfied with their current body image, whereas more than half of African American women were satisfied with their current image.[37]

Additionally, the researchers found that African American men indicated a preference for *larger* body images in African American women than did white men for white women. African American women preferred a slightly larger body image for African American men compared with their white counterparts.

In general, the researchers state that their findings support earlier studies in special populations, suggesting that a social norm may exist on a community-wide level that enables the acceptance of larger body images in African American women.[38] Furthermore, this study suggests that there are ethnic differences in body image concepts that necessitate the development of a better appreciation for and understanding of preferred body images and body types in the African American community.

CONCLUSION

So what conclusion have we derived from this information? The last section of this chapter presented research studies conducted across the United States in varying age- and school-based categories (in elementary school, in middle and high school, in college, and among professional adults). The studies examined the issues of body image and body preference among African American adults, adolescents, and children and found that African Americans to a significant degree select larger body types as the ideal and for self, as compared to whites. The chapter began with the contention that African Americans have a "flexible cultural definition of healthiness" that allows us to appreciate, admire, and emulate larger body types as the cultural norm for males and females.

The results of several studies indicate that African Americans have an ideal body type and preference for body image that differ from those of other groups.[39] In fact, we need to keep in mind positive aspects of African American culture that relate to body image, body type, and body preference. This is well stated by Baskin, Ahluwalia, and Resnicow in their article "Obesity Intervention among African American Children and Adolescents":

Thus, rather than holding whites and majority culture as the ideal, it may be important to incorporate the positive elements of black culture regarding body image and food rather than attempting to shift their values toward those of European Americans.[40]

I wholeheartedly agree with this statement. It is essential that African Americans continue to feel good about our appearance and continue to base our body image within our own culture. Such affirmation will empower us to mentally and physically embrace our individual selves while collectively embracing ourselves as a people.

CHAPTER 4

CULTURAL HISTORICAL REVIEW OF PREFERRED BODY IMAGES AND BODY TYPES

INTRODUCTION

The very moment that Africans arrived in the Americas (1619), they were forced to live in two worlds—in the European American world and in the newly African American world. From that point until President Lincoln issued the Emancipation Proclamation in 1863 (freeing the Africans who lived in the Confederate states that had seceded from the country, but not those in states that remained in the Union), the country's African population was primarily enslaved, although in every state there were some who were not slaves. In general, the period of slavery lasted 244 years—244 years of being forced to live in two worlds, one European American and the other African American.[1]

The major factor for African Americans having this dual identity, dual lifestyle, dual mindset, dual physique, dual body, and dual soul is of course "race." In its very early beginnings, leaders of the New World used *race* as a marker to distinguish various biological and physical differences among two or more populations. Yet leaders in the New World also used race as a sociopolitical tool to control, manipulate, conquer, denigrate, and eradicate another group of people based on their different languages, customs, beliefs, and lifestyles. Although the definition and description of various racial categories have dramatically changed over time in the United States, the negative psychological impact of the terms *race* and *racial category* on all populations—particularly on the African American population—cannot be denied.

For example, *blackness* historically was defined as a demeaned state of being, indicated by skin color or conceptually by blood and genetics. To be

black was to be demeaned by birth and—unlike original sin in the Bible—
it could not be completely redeemed: no absolution through sacrifice or
prayer was available. Blackness was a stain beyond sin. It was an essential
and divine reality, not to be overcome in the eyes of whites through behavior or character, although we, as African Americans, still seemed to believe
that we might overcome it.[2]

Additionally, the physical characteristics of people of African descent and
the objectifying terms given them became equivalent markers in racial discourse; certain derogatory images evoked the same concepts as words like
darkie. Definitions and visual indicators of race were used to form a black-
white hierarchical dialectic in which each was dependent on the other to
support the whole. However, in racial discourse, *black* is the discredited sig-
nifier, and anything connected to this "blackness" was perceived as lesser
than.[3] This was the world that African Americans were brought into, and
this is the world in which we still live.

As Harris states, "the momentum of more than 150 years of derogatory
images and characterizations flowed down on our heads with real consequences because white power enforced and depended on black racial identity." We reinvented ourselves repeatedly to resist and frustrate the
oppressive systems and representations that circumscribed us collectively,
and acted on the belief that we either became co-producers or might change
the worldview by our action. We re-presented ourselves to counter the other
form or representation—the substitute or stand-in—that amounted to a
misrepresentation rather than a proxy.[4]

The gist of this is that images are laden with political and psychological
potential and potency.[5] They help ideological constructions like race take
form in the physical world. They construct, confirm, and affirm identity.
When associated with power, images can impose and reiterate social and
conceptual models on others. Thus, images directly impact one's psychology, and become what one internalizes. Clearly a lot is at stake in visual representation.[6]

Where does this lead us? Harris eloquently states that the black African
body, long a fascination for Europeans because of its difference, served as a
marker facilitating the redefinition of that body as an indicator of a lesser
humanity most suitable for domination and servitude. These ideas were
actualized into a black racial identity that was constructed and reinforced
by convention, religion, ideology, legal institutions, and science.[7]

Therefore, historically some of the most popularized images of African
American men, women, and children were not only incorrect depictions
that were blatantly physically stereotyped, but these were also incorrect
images of how we lived our lives. European American mainstream society
tended to view African Americans in certain visual and physical images and
as living a certain lifestyle—culturally. Africans and African Americans recognized this discourse and made every effort, physically and culturally, to

live in the manner that was, and still is, most comfortable and fitting to their values, beliefs, history—and, of course, to their lifestyle!

EUROPEAN AMERICAN MAINSTREAM SOCIETY'S IMAGES OF AFRICAN AMERICANS, 1790–1920

First and foremost, references in this book to "European American, or American, mainstream society" refer to a network or a group within our society that dictates, controls, and manipulates the majority of society's members to act, think, and behave in a certain manner. This European American, or American, mainstream network used its clout, power, and laws to get the masses (Americans) to believe what it wanted us to believe. Although this European American mainstream network is usually a much smaller segment of the population, it holds the power, the prestige, and the decision making ability to mandate what is right or wrong in American culture.

Some would say that historically, this European American mainstream society network consisted primarily of influential lawmakers, entrepreneurs, and slave owners. Comparatively, some would say that presently this mainstream network has come to consist primarily of influential lawmakers, entrepreneurs, and corporate America. So when this book uses the term *European American, or American, mainstream society*, it is referring to a very select network of people who feel that they hold the beliefs, values, and perceptions for all in our America!

In attempting to provide a detailed and thorough cultural historical account of African American preferred body images and types, we are restricted in the amount of information that has been documented. How can this be the case? Our major source of information, of course, originates from European American art, popular print media, and businesses. Different types of images appeared in these outlets, reaching different audiences, but rarely did any of these images reflect the perspective of the enslaved Africans and new African Americans.[8]

During the nineteenth century, art and popular culture imagery served to both reflect and establish racist ideas and to reiterate the social norms, even when the intentions behind the images were not sinister.[9] African Americans were not imagined visually as full participants in society, so even in sympathetic renderings they were relegated to marginal social roles consistent with the racial reading of the social order. For example, Harris states that William Lloyd Garrison's abolitionist journal *The Liberator* evolved from its initial version, which showed an auction block and the selling of slaves, to one showing the auction block paired with an image of liberation depicting African Americans still doing menial agricultural labor on a plantation, but without a white boss.[10]

These types of images from popular culture became more important and widespread in the second half of the nineteenth century. Images exaggerating simplistic or stereotypical ideas of African Americans were disseminated to large audiences, and these images often used demeaning humor. After the Civil War in particular, demeaning images of blacks had wide distribution through popular media. Along with minstrel shows, they effectively spread stereotypical ideas about African Americans across the country.[11] It is probable that the popularity of minstrels inspired the growth of comic scenarios involving African Americans in print media. The absurdity and cruel satire of minstrel performance was rooted in the imitation of black performance style and in fascination with blackness. Minstrel stereotypes functioned to affirm African Americans' inferiority by giving visual emphasis to physical and cultural differences.[12]

African American Women

Perhaps the most preferred stereotypical image associated with African American women during this period was the *Aunt Jemima* character. This character was created in 1889 to endorse a self-rising pancake mix. After the new owner of the company purchased the Aunt Jemima formula and registered the label, he initiated a search for an African American woman to embody his perception of Aunt Jemima—a Negro woman who might exemplify southern hospitality.[13] This woman, Nancy Green, was found working as a domestic for a judge in Chicago, and she was hired to personify Aunt Jemima. Green traveled throughout the United States promoting the product as a fictional character.[14]

Thus, Aunt Jemima was not a real African American woman, but an invented persona based on European Americans' perceptions of their black servants and on a misinterpretation of a character devised by blacks to critique their own treatment by European Americans. In her commercial incarnation, Aunt Jemima lost the critical commentary found in minstrel performances of the role, and instead was projected entirely the way that European Americans thought of a black cook—as a servile, devoted mammy (itself a fantasy). The coincidence of an innovative marketing strategy that used a live trademark to advertise a revolutionary new product helped to deeply embed Aunt Jemima in the American consciousness.[15]

Interestingly, the physical image associated with the Aunt Jemima character was a heavyset, dark-complected African American woman. The continual dissemination of this imagery of a heavier body type eventually became deeply embedded in the American consciousness. Therefore, the *preferred* and *expected* body type associated with African American women, at least within European American mainstream society, was this heavyset, dark-complected African American woman.

African American Men

Historically, the African male did not have to justify his existence as a human being, nor was he forced to contend with race as a barrier to self-worth. In America, however, African males would be redefined as subhuman property.[16]

African males in America would be forced to live according to European American mainstream society's worldview, which differed dramatically from the one that shaped their lives in Africa.[17] Under slavery, African males no longer had the patriarchal decision-making authority they held in Africa. The ultimate decision maker and patriarchal authority on the plantation was the slave owner and his overseerers.[18]

As with African American women, the major source of information about African American men's physical imagery and body types originated from European American art and popular print media. Often times, negative images of black males were conveyed in stage shows, novels, advertisements, and newspapers. White and Cones III state that in both the North and South, America was saturated with images of clowning, cunning, lazy, ignorant, pleasure-seeking, childlike black men who needed to be supervised and controlled by powerful, competent, and responsible white males.

One of the most pervasive and long-lasting stereotypical images associated with black males during this period was the *Sambo* image.[19] Faithful, loyal, superstitious, dishonest, and always ready to make music, Sambo was another clownlike character who was devoted to his master and had no thought of freedom.[20] The major purpose of this Sambo character, whether in the literature or visually depicted in art, was to convince black males that they belonged within this subordinate caste system, and there was nothing they could do about it.

Another negative physical image of the black male was promoted in the minstrel shows, especially as white minstrels in blackface became very popular in traveling stage shows before the end of slavery. Among the most popular of minstrel performers was Thomas Darmouth Rice, who used the stage name "Daddy Rice." In the 1870s he directed a blackface singing and dancing team known as *Jim Crow*. Jim Crow was famous for its caricatures of black males as dimwitted, ridiculous-sounding, shuffling, dancing, happy-go-lucky, irresponsible creatures.[21]

Supported by science and religion and the popular European American mainstream culture of the day, images of black male inferiority proved to have a deep and lasting impact. White and Cones III state that what started out as a social construct created by a certain segment of European American society came to be predominantly reified as a virtual reality believed in, in some fashion, by most European Americans in all sections of the country. They further state that as the stereotypical images of black males were handed down from generation to generation, they became frozen in the public mind as an accurate representation of a material and physical reality.[22]

It therefore becomes quite apparent that culturally and historically, African Americans had very little opportunity to express or document what they preferred with respect to physical beauty for women, physical traits for men, and overall preferred body types. African Americans regarded the black stereotyped images from European American mainstream society with a complex fusion of credibility, ambivalence, and outright disbelief that failed to provide clear distinction between caricature and reality.[23] It was thus this discourse and disconnect from European American mainstream society that caused a majority of African Americans to not only reject these negative stereotypic images of physical beauty and traits, but also to reconnect with their own unique ethnic beauty and physical attributes.

AFRICAN AMERICAN PHYSICAL IMAGE: THE CULTURAL IMPACT OF HAIR ON CONCEPTS OF BEAUTY, 1790–1920

Perhaps the element of preferred physical appearance and image that we, as African Americans, have most consistently been able to accentuate and express culturally since arriving in the New World is our *hair*. In African cultures the grooming and styling of hair have long been important social rituals. Elaborate hair designs reflecting tribal affiliation, status, sex, age, occupation, and the like were common, and the cutting, shaving, wrapping, and braiding of hair were centuries-old arts.[24] Typically, the hair of eighteenth-century West Africans was not bushy or unkempt. Women from these areas, using braiding and wrapping techniques, had their hair arranged in highly elaborate configurations, whereas West African men generally cut their hair rather short.[25] In part, it was the texture of African hair that allowed these cultural practices to develop.

Not surprisingly, in the slave systems of the New World, African Americans lacked both the time to practice such elaborate hairstyling and the implement with which to perform it—for example, the African pick, or comb, whose long, smooth teeth would not snag or tear thick, tightly curled hair. Yet slave owners' descriptions of runaways show clearly that the hair of large numbers of slaves remained sufficiently malleable to be styled in surprisingly elaborate ways.[26]

Nonetheless, as the years passed, African Americans desired and needed new methods and materials for their hair care. At the turn of the twentieth century, two African American businesswomen—Annie Turnbo Malone and Madame C. J. Walker—developed and built their businesses by selling hair care products to black women.[27] In particular, Madame C. J. Walker developed a new method of relaxing hair and promoting its health.

Madame C. J. Walker was born Sarah Breedlove in Delta, Louisiana, on 23 December 1867. Her parents, Owen and Minerva Breedlove, and five older siblings—Lovenia, Owen, Junior, Alexander, and James—were share-croppers on a cotton plantation named Grand View. Sarah was the first member of the family to be born free, just a few days shy of the fifth anniversary of the signing of the Emancipation Proclamation.[28]

As A'Lelia Bundles, the great-great-granddaughter of Madame C. J. Walker, reports in her book *On Her Own Ground: The Life and Times of Madam C. J. Walker*, Sarah left home at age fourteen with Moses McWilliams (most likely her common-law husband). On 6 June 1885, between Sarah's seventeenth and eighteenth birthdays, she gave birth to a daughter, Lelia. Unfortunately, Moses died three years later, leaving Sarah to raise Lelia by herself. "I was left a widow at the age of twenty with a lit-tle girl to raise," she is quoted to have said.[29] A photograph of Sarah taken at this time is described as follows:

She was a physically attractive young woman. While any clothing she owned surely was worn, even shabby, her waist had begun to contour between a full bosom and rounded hips. Her chestnut-brown body was firm from field work, her forearm mus-cles thickened and defined from the washboard. A heart-shaped face framed alert ebony eyes, slightly flared nostrils, and purposeful lips. As with so many other black women who had long forgotten the elaborate grooming rituals of their African ancestors, her crudely braided hair was usually covered with a patterned head wrap.[30]

By 1889 Sarah and three-year-old Lelia headed north to St. Louis, where Sarah's brothers lived. Interestingly, her brothers owned a very successful barbershop. They were among the nearly three hundred black barbers in St. Louis at this time who were considered the best in the city, and who made up the largest group of black entrepreneurs. Although most barbers did not become wealthy, they enjoyed more independence than laborers, servants, teamsters, messengers, and porters—the jobs then held by most black men.[31]

As Sarah and Lelia settled into the African American community of St. Louis, an interesting phenomenon was occurring throughout the United States. In a society that denied legal rights and economic opportunities on the basis of race and gender, Sarah and other women endured daily emo-tional and psychological pressure to assimilate by minimizing the physical reminders of slavery.[32] No matter how beautiful, how well groomed, or how stylish she may have managed to make herself look, Sarah would never meet America's standard of beauty. At the turn of the twentieth century this standard was the Gibson Girl.

According to Bundles, this "ideal American girl," with her chic, haughty, and graceful pose, was in part distinguished by long, silky tresses artfully arranged beneath the brim of her beribboned hat. The faultless Gibson

Look, attempted by women of any race or class, seemed most easily attained with the artist's ink pen. Bundles further states

Most black women, and certainly Sarah, were hard-pressed to twist their full lips into a dainty Cupid's bow. That the tightly nipped Gibson torso was physically impossible to sustain for any woman who needed to exhale did not prevent American women from attempting the impossible.[33]

The effect of this Gibson Girl image, and the high value that European American mainstream society placed on straight hair and white skin, greatly influenced Sarah to find a way to better appreciate her brown skin and curly, coiled hair. Not long after, Sarah made the discovery that changed her entire life and greatly changed the way thousands of African American women perceived their own beauty.

"When I made my discovery, I had no idea of placing it on the market for the benefit of others; I was simply in search of something that would save or restore my own hair," Sarah explained.[34] Further, she considered the miraculous concoction to be "an inspiration from God," designed for her to "place in the reach of those who appreciate beautiful hair and healthy scalps, which is the glory of woman."

The success of Sarah's scalp treatment—not only in growing hair but also in curing the scalp disease experienced by many black women at the time—made her an overnight success. A few years later, after marrying businessman C. J. Walker in 1906, Madame C. J. Walker and her husband officially launched her beauty hair care products nationally.

Madame C. J. Walker launched a national advertising campaign in 1906 with an ad featuring three photographs of herself. The middle photo is in a rectangular box, and the two on either side are ovals. The middle photo is of a young Walker with her hair pulled back over the ears and the hair in front styled in curls over the forehead. Her hair looks about three to four inches long and the words "Before Using" are superimposed over the bottom of the box. The two oval photographs on either side picture an older Walker looking directly into the camera with long hair falling well below her shoulders.[35]

According to Noliwe Rooks, the "before" photograph suggests that short hair interfered with Walker's sense of self-worth to the extent that she could not look the world (or here, the camera) in the eye. However, once Walker's hair has grown long, she looks boldly into the camera. Hair growth has altered her sense of self. In this way, "before" and "after" take on ideological significance, as Walker illustrates for readers that hair growth is key to feelings of defiance and resistance.[36]

The impact of this first ad campaign, along with an eighteen-month tour of the South that she took with her husband, C. J., allowed Madame Walker to connect with African American women. Together, they were fellow sufferers struggling with problems that her hair care product would cure. With believers wanting to know more about her products, Madame Walker soon started training women in their use.

Madame Walker considered the ritual of her system to be as important as the actual hairstyle. She instructed her agents to create an atmosphere in which their clients would feel pampered and valued while their hair was being given proper attention. Indeed, agents interested in the Walker system of treatment learned a philosophy of inner, as well as outer, beauty.[37]

Within a few years, Madame Walker had completely established herself as not only the leading and wealthiest entrepreneur of black women's hair care products and treatments, but she had also become a leader in social and political arenas as well. After divorcing C. J. and settling in Indianapolis, Madame Walker and her daughter Lelia became symbols of success in African American communities across the country.

With Madame Walker's success, many other African American women ventured into the same line of hair care and beauty products, and enjoyed success themselves. Rooks notes an interesting cultural pattern that occurred during this period when African American women began to advertise their products.

African American women who advertised beauty products produced cultural images that served to re-present the bodies of other women whose race they shared. In the process, they articulated standards of beauty that were not predicated on unfavorable racial ideologies that structured and undergirded discourses from competing advertising concerns. They drew upon culturally discrete symbols and practices within African American communities and placed African American women's bodies within the context of religious doctrine, which dictated that a woman should strive to have long hair. They also argued that hairdressing was a career choice African American women could ill afford to overlook.[38]

From the 1920s onward, the hair care business has provided opportunities for African American women to gain a small measure of independence by selling hair care services in their homes or in small beauty shops.[39] Although the businesses were small, they provided an alternative to domestic work and helped African American women to establish their own standard of beauty.

Overall, the impact of "hair"—African American women's hair in particular—helped to reshape and reorient the definition of what constitutes beauty and what are the preferred body types within the African American community. Advertising hair products offered African American women the opportunity to shape identities, to broaden representations of those identities, to communicate culturally specific meanings of the significance of those identities, and, by extension, to place African American women within American and African American culture. Thus, hair offers an opportunity to examine the politics of African American women's bodies and the representation of those bodies to African American women.[40]

AFRICAN AMERICAN PHYSICAL IMAGE: THE CULTURAL IMPACT OF BEAUTY PAGEANTS AND CONTESTS, 1890–1950

Another feature of African American culture that allowed us to express our physical, outward uniqueness as a people was the beauty pageant. The complex history of black beauty pageant stretches back over a century in which black institutions variously ignored, addressed, incorporated, contested, or rejected European American mainstream standards of beauty and European American depictions of African Americans. Accounts of African American beauty pageants, which predated attempts to integrate all-white contests, can be found in the black press as early as the 1890s. Articles on black beauty pageants reported sponsorship by the music industry that promoted black entertainers, and by black newspapers, black cosmetics and hair care companies, fraternal orders, social clubs, the NAACP, and institutions of higher education. The pageants varied according to whether they were explicitly framed as displays of racial pride, whether they incorporated images of Africa or Europe, whether they promoted explicitly middle-class images of women, and whether they challenged or reinforced the diversity of pigmentation within the African American population.[41] What is certain about these numerous black beauty pageants around the country was their assertion that black women are beautiful.

Beauty pageants projected ideal images of African American women—ideals shaped by a particularly male-dominated, middle-class, black worldview. Middle-class black men, as journalists and community leaders, played a greater role than women as spokespersons for African Americans. Middle-class black women had significant leadership roles within circumscribed areas, but men dominated the wider black public arena. From editorial pages and podiums they called on women to embody particular definitions of black womanhood. Interestingly, the record of black beauty pageants is thus very often a narrative of how black men, as cultural agents, constructed black women as cultural symbols.[42]

For example, as Maxine Craig highlights in her book *Ain't I a Beauty Queen: Black Women, Beauty, and the Politics of Race*, in 1891 the black Chicago newspaper the *Appeal* launched a beauty contest. To announce the contest the newspaper asked, "Who Is the Most Beautiful Afro-American Woman?" and solicited participation from its readers. The contest was open to "every Colored woman in America" and was primarily a gimmick to build circulation.[43] Well, the gimmick worked! The *Appeal's* assumption that its entirely African American readership would be eager to honor the beauty of the women in their lives attests to the ability of African Americans to maintain a sense of their own worthiness.[44]

By contrast, the competition sponsored by the *New York Age* was promoted as a way to fight debased images of black women. Yet after receiving a letter from one of its influential readers, the *New York Age* decided to find the ideal American Negro woman from among submitted photographs of beauties. Interestingly, the ideal American Negro woman was described as having

a well balanced and symmetrical head, full slender neck, the features clear cut, with the appearance of being chiseled rather than cast; the forehead broad and slightly expansive, a fine Negro nose with a trace of Egyptian and a slight aquiline curve; the mouth fairly small but well proportioned and a slightly pointed, round, firm chin; the eyes should be large but slightly elongated; surmounted by a fine brow that is not too sharp, delicately arched, and last but not least, with the marvelously fine curving eyelash of which the Negro race can be just proud.[45]

Craig describes this "trace of Egyptian" in the ideal American Negro woman as reflecting primarily middle-class black men's fascination with Egypt. By having Egypt represent the African in the American Negro, the *Age* was responding directly to racist descriptions of American blacks as barbarians. Egypt evoked images of grand civilizations of great wealth. In the popular imagination, the remainder of Africa was merely the jungle home of backward people. Guided by the popular social mapping of the continent of Africa, the *Age* claimed Egyptian ancestry for its ideal Negro woman.[46]

After months of buildup in the pages of the newspaper, the *Age* selected the "Chosen Fifteen" beauties. On a Friday night in October 1914 at the Manhattan Casino, the judges announced the "Chosen Fifteen" and presented local winners with solid gold "One of the Chosen Fifteen" pins. Photographs of the winners were displayed in the casino and reproduced on the front page of the *Age*. Not surprisingly, the winners were all light-skinned women.[47]

The controversy surrounding these early national black beauty contests did not dissuade local organizers from sponsoring their own black beauty pageants. Throughout the 1920s fraternal groups such as the Knights of Pythias sponsored pageants; in black enclaves in the North, migrants from Louisiana crowned Mardi Gras beauty queens; and black newspapers continued to boost sales by combining themes of racial pride with the publication of photographs of beauties.[48]

Yet it was another controversial black beauty pageant that challenged African Americans' standard of beauty. In 1947 Harlem's Golden Gate Ballroom sponsored the Miss Fine Brown Frame contest, hosted by Buddy Johnson—the band leader who made a musical hit of "Miss Fine Brown Frame." Although contest judges originally chose a light-complexioned woman as the winner, audience displeasure influenced them to reevaluate their selection. They later awarded Evelyn Sanders—a curvaceous, dark-complexioned woman—the winning title of "Miss Fine Brown Frame."

Ebony magazine reported on the contest and described Sanders as the darkest among a decade of Harlem beauty queens and the most "exotic"—a pairing of black skin tone with brazen sexuality. She was a natural woman of the people who sewed her own daring bikini, loved to eat, and eschewed exercise and cosmetics. Simply put, Sanders won on the basis of her body.[49]

This brief overview of the black beauty pageants—from the late 1800s to the mid-1900s—demonstrates the multitude of cultural rankings available within black communities. The pageants were the product of black institutions, and provided strong evidence that we, African Americans, prized our own African beauty. By their very existence, the pageants countered depictions of African American women as ugly or indecent. The culture produced by the black middle class, as displayed in its beauty contests, was never a simple replica of the dominant culture, which itself was heterogeneous. As an institution of the black community, the pageants were neither fully autonomous nor fully dominated. They incorporated but also altered the prevailing discourse of race, gender, and class.[50]

Additionally, the pageants conveyed, altered, and reinforced standards of beauty, and shifted the cultural orientation of black identity toward the allure of the ancient Nile, the glamour of Europe, the citizenship of America, or the entire continent of Africa. They promoted particular class orientations. Although light-complexioned women won most contests for many years, their victories represented only a partial view of the valuation of black women in black communities.[51]

CONCLUSION

One of the major challenges in describing the cultural history of a people is collecting enough historical documents, monographs, articles, or archived journals to describe the events of a particular time in history. Once the necessary documents are collected, organized, and interpreted, then a vivid cultural historical picture can be formulated and presented.

For this chapter on the cultural history of African American preferred body images and types, very little historical information has been written or documented in even the slightest sense. Historical references to African American body images and types often had their origin in art or the popular media, where all too often the descriptions were heavily stereotypical.

Thus another major challenge in describing the cultural history of a people is to achieve a good balance of historical documentation. The desired balance requires historical documentation that is recorded by both those observing the lifestyles of another people, and by the people themselves. For this chapter, accurate historical documentation of the African American lifestyle has required input from African Americans themselves.

This is the major reason this chapter presents two perspectives on African American body images and body types—one as regarded by

European American mainstream society and one regarded from the African American perspective. Both perspectives are significant and historically important in that they allow us to see how far apart we sometimes are in describing the history of a people and which historical issues—ranging from hair care to beauty pageants—are culturally connected to the overall physical imagery of African American body images and body types.

African American Body Types and the Fashion Industry

INTRODUCTION

This chapter begins with a set of questions to help readers truly "feel" the cultural complexity of this issue—African Americans and the fashion industry:

- How can a people who have been denied their ethnic heritage and identity become part of a fashion industry that consistently overlooks their unique qualities and strengths?
- How can a people determine what is fashionable when they have always been left out or denied the opportunity to develop fashion for themselves?
- Do African American body types need a specific type of fashion to accentuate their physical attributes?
- Who determines the fashion styles for African Americans?
- Why is fashion important to African Americans?
- Why has European American mainstream society felt the need to determine the fashion style for African Americans?
- When did African Americans begin to take charge of their own fashion?
- Why do African Americans feel that they need to express their fashion style differently than European Americans?

To reiterate, these questions need to be asked up front so that we can not only answer these very important questions, but so that we can also recognize the phenomenal journey that African Americans experienced in the fashion industry.

Now that those questions have been presented, let us clearly establish to what we are referring when we speak of the fashion industry. Fashion is defined as "the current style or custom, as in dress or behavior; the mode for the present."[1] Fashion is a public presentation of the body in which cultural preferences determine how it is visually displayed and which body types (women's and men's) are selected to display the latest fashionable designs. Therefore, fashion truly reflects our attitudes, beliefs, values, and cultural preferences for certain types of clothing and certain types of people who model the clothing.

In the fashion industry, African American fashion models were some of the first to expand the definition of beauty and to see the effects of that expanded definition. They helped to stretch a new canvas and expand the palette, but neither the picture nor the frame would change overnight.[2]

In particular, the early professional models of color in the 1940s were often light-skinned with European features, deviating only slightly from the European American ideal. Barbara Summers (2001), a former African American fashion model, stated the following about the difficulties that black models had in breaking into the fashion model industry:

Black models are living proof that beauty is more than skin deep. From the past to the present, their unique flair and impeccable style won them a place no social legislation could create or deny. Each step onto the runway, each click of the camera gave real form to what was only an abstraction. With each distinctive face, figure, and personality, they focused our awareness on their presence as individuals and their significance as a group. Whether they knew it or not, they were on a mission to redefine beauty and power. It was a mission that, in its own way, would change the world.[3]

AFRICAN AMERICAN FASHION: EARLY YEARS, 1920s–1950s

Nowhere does it become more apparent that African Americans live in two worlds than when we look at the fashion industry. The fashion industry reflects African Americans' discourse with European American mainstream society because African Americans had to create their own separate fashion culture and establish a system and structure for maintaining their particular type of fashion. Once this African American fashion system was in place by the early 1900s, African American fashion took off! Increasingly from the mid-1920s, black media attention became focused not on beauty contests, but on African American fashion parades. These parades were related institutions that also relied on the display of black female bodies, but would prove to have more cultural force and staying power.[4]

Starting in the early years of the twentieth century, department stores hosted fashion shows, and these had immediately proved successful. By the late 1910s and 1920s, the stores were putting on style shows organized by more than one establishment, screening fashion movies, and staging huge fashion pageants replete with models, an orchestra, and special effects. Although African Americans were not excluded by law from attending these mainstream department stores, they were however not welcomed. Yet African Americans found a way to participate in fashion through a set of black institutions that paralleled those of European American mainstream society.[5]

For example, in Chicago, Professor Clark, who ran a dancing school, rented the Masonic Hall and ran a style show featuring "a large number of beautifully gowned women"; in Philadelphia, Idell Robinson displayed the work of her dressmaking students in a fashion show at the Waltz Dream Academy; in New York, leading tailor R. R. Burt staged a "Midnight Fashion Show" at the Lafayette, one of Harlem's most famous theatres; and in Brooklyn, the Monday Circle held a "fashion promenade" in Arcadia Hall for the benefit of the Lincoln Settlement.[6]

As with the black beauty contest, which was becoming popular at the same time, the success of small, often local, events encouraged organization on a larger scale. In Chicago, the Annual Fashion Show for the benefit of the YWCA was inaugurated in 1923. White and White state that a reporter for *Half Century,* present at the second of these functions, commented on the "brilliant array of beautiful women on the stage, displaying the newest in hats, gowns and furs to an audience arrayed in creations worthy of more than passing note," and surmised that the obvious success of that year's event meant that "its permanency is assured."[7]

The growing popularity of fashion shows provided African American newspapers with a further opportunity to display attractive young black women. During the spring of 1926, the *Pittsburgh Courier* supplied its readers, in rapid succession, with photographs of dozens of models under headlines such as "Chicago Maids and Matrons Exhibit What is Proper in the Spring Mode," "Missouri Maids Exhibit the Latest in Feminine Foibles," "California Proves that Clothes Do Not Make The Woman, But Oh! How They Proclaim Her," "Pretty New Orleans Maids Know How to Wear 'Em," and "Leaders and Models in Louisville Style Revue."[8]

As these captions indicate, the fashion show quickly spread across America, even into the South. When plans for the first Crescent City Style Show, held in April 1926, were released, the organizers reassured New Orlean's African Americans that it would be "similar in all respects to those shows of the East and North." The show, featuring over 300 local African Americans and climaxing with a wedding scene, was a huge success.[9]

By the mid 1930s, not only were the fashion shows flourishing on many levels, but they also became cultural extravaganzas. In New York in April 1935, the Twenty-Third Utopia Fashion Show took place at the Renaissance Casino. That same month, at the League Building in Flushing, the Corona Progressive Republican Club staged what was described as "one of the

North Shore's leading social events" featuring "charming manikins" wearing the newest spring fashions. In early June, the O. Clay Maxwell Club of the Mount Olive Baptist Church on Lenox Avenue held its annual fashion show displaying spring and summer styles. In addition, other affairs were much more commercial, featuring the latest department store fashion ware.[10]

The reasons for the success of the fashion shows are seen in the number of press accounts of these events. White and White stated that if beauty contests were a novelty, emblematic of a new interest in the black body and of the modernist impulse, fashion parades and fashion itself became the means by which the African American middle class defined itself.[11]

Interestingly, as African Americans increasingly moved to the cities, particularly the black middle class, they rapidly assumed control of the burgeoning fashion show industry and used it to establish themselves as the authority on what respectable blacks should wear and thus to differentiate themselves from ordinary working-class African Americans. Fashion parades, sponsored by middle-class clubs and charities, organized by respectable society matrons, and using debutantes or society women as mannequins, set a standard for members of the middle class to emulate. Newspaper and magazine coverage of these events and of fashion itself, which hinted at a glamorous, even opulent lifestyle, gave everyone else something to envy.[12]

White and White contend that the fashion parade must have also struck a particular chord with African Americans, echoing as it did a key black institution dating back to slavery times. In some senses, the black fashion parade constituted a more stagy and contrived variation of the Sunday promenade to and from church that was always a part of African American life in both the North and the South. Both were spectacles in which participants expressed themselves and desired their peers and "inferiors" to notice them. Both were didactic rituals deliberately and clearly establishing social differences. It was this connection with African American cultural history that allowed the African American fashion parade to combine ostentation and piety, consumption and religion (church groups and charities were the usual organizers and beneficiaries) in a way that sanctioned the cultural authority not only of the fashion show institution but of the black middle class itself.[13]

Interestingly, what was most important about the early African American fashion parades and shows during this time period was the public declaration that the *black body* was capable of being regarded as a thing of *beauty*. Against an unvarying background of demeaning visual portrayals of African American bodies in cartoons, magazine illustrations, advertisements, and film, black beauty contests and fashion shows were not merely vivid repudiations of black physical and aesthetic inferiority but salutary expressions of African American pride.[14]

Furthermore, White and White emphasize the following:

The fact that for the first time blacks were being presented, through the contests and fashion shows themselves and the widespread publicity given to these events by the African American press, in what was, by contemporary standards, an unambiguously positive way.[15]

AFRICAN AMERICANS IN EUROPEAN AMERICAN MAINSTREAM SOCIETY'S FASHION INDUSTRY: EARLY YEARS TO THE PRESENT

Although African Americans were highly successful in creating and maintaining their own fashion shows and parades on a national and local level at the turn of the twentieth century and in decades to follow, they were not able to participate on a regular and substantial basis in the European American mainstream society's fashion industry in any major capacity.

Ironically, pioneering African American dressmakers such as Elizabeth Keckly, who was Mrs. Mary Lincoln's (wife of President Lincoln) dressmaker during the 1860s; and Ann Cole Lowe, who created fashions for the nation's leading political and entertainment families during the 1950s and 1960s, particularly the wedding dress of Jackie Bouvier Kennedy (wife of President John F. Kennedy) did not convince the European American mainstream fashion industry to open their doors for other African Americans. Even in the world of fashion modeling and acting, Josephine Baker (actress, model, singer) and Lena Horne (actress, singer, model) could not break down the walls of denial. Despite the early contributions of a number of outstanding African American models (e.g., Ophelia DeVore, Dorothea Towles, Helen Williams, and Mozella Roberts) in the European American mainstream fashion industry in the United States (dressmakers and models), a vast majority of African American dressmakers, designers and models simply did not have continual access to this larger fashion industry.[16]

According to Barbara Summers, former African American model, the foremost authority on the history of black models, and author of *Skin Deep: Inside the World of Black Fashion Models* and *Black and Beautiful: How Women of Color Changed the Fashion Industry*, the big breakthrough for African American models in the European American mainstream fashion industry occurred in 1973. For black models, the defining moment of change took place at Versailles, France, on a date to remember: November 28, 1973. For the first time, a group of African American models—no longer isolated, individual stars—walked off an unusually opulent runway and onto the pages of history.[17]

This event occurred at the stage of the Opera House in the Sun King's imperial chateau. To celebrate the restoration of Louis XIV's 300-year-old palace, five American fashion designers were invited to show their work along with five French couturiers. The French team of designers consisted of Pierre Cardin, Christian Dior, Hubert de Givenchy, Yves Saint Laurent, and Emmanuel Ungaro. The American team of designers consisted of Bill Blass, Stephen Burrows, Halston, Anne Klein, and Oscar de la Renta, who were well known to the fashion-conscious of the States, but not known internationally.[18]

After all the other models completed their fashion runway strut for the crowd, the African American fashion models were ready to take the stage. Interestingly even the American designers did not realize that they had a secret weapon during this event—black women. African American women were the surprise element, the shock troops on the runway. Billie Blair, Alva Chinn, Pat Cleveland, Norma Jean Darden, Charlene Dash, Bethann Hardison, Barbara Jackson, Ramona Saunders, and Amina Warsuma were among the two dozen mannequins selected to present the work of the American designers.[19]

These women of all shades of beauty brought their own special qualities to the work. In the words of one long-time fashion show director, they epitomized "spirit, energy, personality, music. The clothes were moving. Those Girls made that audience come alive. It was electric, exciting."[20]

Summers (2001) highlights the comments of a couple of reports of the event:

The most dramatic moment came when Betham Hardison stalked down the runway in a tight-fitting yellow silk halter by Burrows holding a floor-length train by a tiny ring on her pinky.

When Hardison reached center stage, she made a dramatic turn and haughtily dropped her train. The audience exploded in a frenzy of approval. They stomped, screamed and tossed their programs into the air.

The bejeweled Paris audience was stunned by the showmanship of the black models from America (as well as with the no-fuss backgrounds and elegant wearability of the American sportswear). The Parisian aristocrats were both frightened and thrilled.[21]

Sadly, however, Summers emphasizes that while the African American models were indeed the stars of the show, their reward was little more than symbolic. After enduring "tears, fights, prima donna trips by both models and designers and 11 hours of rehearsing without food and little water,"[22] they had some priceless memories, but little else. The models were in fact discussing the formation of a union to upgrade their working conditions and improve their pay. The actual reality was that these fabulous performers received less than fabulous sums of twenty-five dollars per day for spending money and three hundred dollars in salary for the show.[23]

Nonetheless, this event at Versailles in 1973 changed the way American designers incorporated African American models into their fashion shows as well as how the international fashion designers and audiences viewed the African American women's style, energy, beauty, and body type.

Quite naturally, after this phenomenal fashion show, images of black beauty began to move into the mainstream of American and, thus, world culture on a monthly basis. Black models had to develop a stronger style and project a stronger image. They already stood out. To become the best in the business they had to become outstanding. Whether they were born with the instinct for style or whether they learned it on the job, black models were obliged to make themselves better than good.[24]

No one model was more representative of her era than Naomi Sims. She personified the slogan "Black is Beautiful" with equal emphasis on deep color and high value. None of the models during the 1960s was as tall or as dark. Naomi was the first to prove that dark black was unquestionably beautiful, unexpectedly exciting, challenging, desirable, and profitable.[25]

Naomi enjoyed unprecedented recognition and success. Although, by her color alone, she was considered revolutionary, and by her size, strictly high fashion, she made important forays into all sectors of America via the magazine covers of *Ladies' Home Journal, McCalls, Life, Cosmopolitan,* and *Vogue.*[26]

With the incredible success of Naomi Sims in mainstream American fashion and fashion magazines, it was just a matter of time before the influx of other African American models hit the front covers. *Glamour* magazine found its first African American cover model in Katiti Kironde II and then later followed up with Daphne Maxwell—a freckle-nosed African American college student. In addition, the first model of color on *Mademoiselle's* cover was Jolie Jones—the green-eyed daughter of music celebrity Quincy Jones.[27]

From the 1970s to the present, there has been a virtual explosion of African American models working successfully in European American mainstream fashion and fashion magazines. Summers (2001) highlights a number of African American models during this time period and here are just a few of their names:

Darnella Thomas, Sherry Brewer, Toukie Smith, Carol LaBrie, Nancy Clark, Sandi Bass, Lynn Watts, Jade Brown, Veronica Webb, Paulette James, Judy Gillett, Anna Fiona, Terri Coleman, Barbara Bennett, Sandra Stevens, Beverly Johnson, Louise Vyent, Lana Ogilvie, Jolie Jones, Billie Blair, Sheila Anderson, Karen Alexander, Roshumba, Peggy Dillard, Naomi Campbell, and Iman.[28]

Not only did these African American models have successful careers in the European American mainstream fashion industry, they helped to diversify the image of beauty associated with African Americans and Americans in general. In fact, each one of the African American fashion models had their own unique look, persona, style, skin color, hair style, and body type.

Perhaps the subtle impact of these diverse African American fashion models enabled more Americans to open up to the fact that an African American woman can actually represent "American beauty." Well, that fact came true when Vanessa L. Williams became the first African American woman to be crowned Miss America in 1983.

Yet it was one particular African American fashion model that completely changed the "physical image" and "standard body type" of an American fashion model. That African American fashion model is Tyra Banks.

After Tyra Banks graduated from Immaculate Heart High School in Los Angeles, instead of proceeding directly to college to study film and television production as she had planned, she decided to see some of the world and give modeling a try. After being rejected by several modeling agencies, Elite Model Management finally gave the 17-year-old Tyra her first modeling job.

Within Banks' first week in Paris, other designers were so entranced by her presence on the runway that she was booked for an unprecedented twenty-five shows—a record in the business for a newcomer. According to Summers, what made Tyra stand out even more amongst all the other elite models was that "Tyra had the tawny coloring, curvaceous sexuality, and hip, humorous attitude that put her in demand by designers, photographers, and directors."[29]

Later in the 1990s, Tyra Banks completed extensive print and runway work for all the major fashion giants. Throughout these years, she appeared on countless numbers of fashion, health, and lifestyle magazine covers. In fact, Tyra was the first African American woman on the covers of *GQ, Sports Illustrated Swimsuit Issue,* and *Victoria's Secret* catalog—all mainstream American magazines.

Yet Tyra was determined to redefine the nature of a model's career. A woman no longer simply modeled and then moved on to another life. She hired her mother to be her manager and then set up her own corporation. Along with her early acting gigs on TV shows and then movies, Tyra and her Los Angeles-based company, Bankable Productions, developed the hit reality show *America's Next Top Model* in 2003 and then a couple of years later launched her own successful talk show, *The Tyra Banks Show.*

Additionally, Tyra Banks' charitable organization centers on a leadership program for young girls called TZONE. It is designed to reinforce core values of trust and support; challenge teen girls to resist negative social pressures; and enhance self-empowerment, inspiring girls to become confident leaders in their communities.

Recently, *Ebony Magazine* celebrated African American contribution to the fashion industry and in the article titled "The Fickle Business of Fashion: According to Tyra, Iman, Kimora and Alek." The magazine praised Tyra's career in the following manner: "Banks' reinvention as a TV impresario embodies how fashion, and by extension her image, have been democratized. Once an elite model, Banks now earns a living bringing fashion—and herself—to the masses."[30]

Finally in this section, we must include the impact of a couple of more current celebrity fashion model-actresses. Specifically, two celebrities who are highly respected and who have a very large following in the fashion industry and African American community are Kimora Lee Simmons and Tracee Ellis Ross.

Kimora Lee Simmons is president and creative director of Baby Phat—a clothing line and lifestyle brand for the glamorous woman who is all things hip-hop and everything fashion. She was married to Russell Simmons—a major business entertainment entrepreneur in the hip-hop world—and has two daughters from the marriage.

Kimora is of Korean and African American heritage and became a model at the age of thirteen, when she was awarded an exclusive modeling contract with Chanel. Just after her fourteenth birthday, she left for Paris to work under the tutelage of famed Chanel designer Karl Lagerfield. She quickly gained attention in the fashion world when Lagerfield closed his haute couture show with Simmons.[31]

In 2007, Kimora Lee Simmons published a book titled *Fabulosity,* a concept which she defines as a state of everything that is a fabulous. The five key components to her fabulosity philosophy are confidence, uniqueness, independence, luxury, and generosity.[32]

What is particularly noteworthy of Simmons' book is that she directly addresses the issues of image and body and her ethnicity. She states:

Body image has this huge hold on women's minds today and to me, worrying about and hating on yourself is not fabulous. It's not being free. The twisted thing is that the people who are rewarded for their physiques are often not the ones who worked hardest on them. I think we should embrace the fact that we're all different shapes and all need to be the healthiest we can be, and then give props to those who keep themselves fighting fit![33]

Kimora also talks about her ethnicity in relationship to her standard of beauty—Korean and African American. She states:

When I was younger doing the collections, my ethnic features were always a challenge. I didn't have an eyelid and no makeup artist knew how to do my face. I used to cry—I felt humiliated! But now I realize it's better to have this ethnic mix. There's a lot of drama in highlighting your unique features. It's exciting to see women playing up their unique features; it makes the world a richer place! And it shifts the beauty standard by several degrees so that exotic and unusual features become the norm. Personally, my goal is one day to not just be seen as an icon of ethnic beauty, but as an icon of beauty, period. That'll mean diversity has really been embraced.[34]

Tracee Ellis Ross is another celebrity model-actress who continues to have a major influence on the issues related to body image and beauty in the African American community. Ross is an NAACP Image award winning actress for her role in the successful long-running TV series, *Girlfriends*.

Tracee Ellis Ross, daughter of singer-actress Diana Ross, graduated from Brown University and worked in the fashion industry as a model and contributing fashion editor to *Mirabella* and *New York*. As a model, Ross was featured in national advertising campaigns, including those for Gap, The Donna Karan Collection, Paul Mitchell, and DKNY. She was also the cover girl in the Fall 2006 edition of the magazine *Vibe Vixen*.[35]

In 2005, Tracee Ellis Ross contributed her straightforward comments to the book *Naked: Black Women Bare All About Their Skin, Hair, Hips, Lips, and Other Parts*. This book featured candid, witty, insightful and provocative comments from today's African American women about their bodies—from head to toe. Ross states the following about her body:

Really though, there was nothing I could do. No matter how small I got, how much I worked out, my proportions stayed the same. Eventually I faced the inevitable—this was the body and the booty I was given, and I might as well start loving them. I've stopped wasting time trying to hide my tush. It's not like I wear clothes to accentuate it, but I have the type of tush that is pretty obvious no matter what. Being too skinny no longer makes me happy. Instead, I like my body when I have a booty. I feel sexy and more womanly. I feel substantial.[36]

AFRICAN AMERICAN MAINSTREAM SOCIETY'S FASHION INDUSTRY: THE EBONY FASHION FAIR

Currently celebrating its fiftieth year, Ebony Fashion Fair is still the premier fashion event in black communities nationwide. Margena Christian, features editor for *JET Magazine*, offers the following analyis on the "History" page on Ebony Fashion Fair's Web site:

Attending Ebony Fashion Fair is always quite an experience. Noted for the eye-catching, jaw-dropping designs, the show has been credited with helping Black women to keep up with what's vogue across the Atlantic. . . . The show has also been noted for its bold outfits [for women and men] that celebrate the human body. It's nothing to see sheer camisoles and blouses that reveal breasts, pants that expose the buttocks, or evening gowns with splits so high they become the talk of the fashion show. And while many of the creations appeared "wild" back then and even now, it seems that the show is well ahead of its time.[37]

Earlier in the article, Christian recounts the history of the event:

It all started in 1956 when the idea for the Ebony Fashion Fair was conceived. In an effort to support a worthy cause, Mrs. Jessie Covington Dent, wife of Dr. Albert W. Dent, former president emeritus of Dillard University in New Orleans, approached Mr. John H. Johnson, publisher, chairman, and CEO of Johnson Publishing Company, to sponsor a mini-fashion show fund-raiser for the Women's Auxiliary of Flint-Goodrich Hospital in New Orleans.

The first show was such a success that Mr. Johnson, in consultation with Mrs. [Eunice] Johnson [now producer and director of Ebony Fashion Fair] and Freda C. DeKnight, home service director, then decided to take it on a cross-country tour to benefit other worthy charities. Ten cities were selected in 1958 by Mr. and Mrs. Johnson to host the first Ebony Fashion Fair. With the theme "Ebony Fashion Fair Around the Clock," the show featured four female models with DeKnight serving as commentator. Ticket prices ranged from $3.50 to $12. The prices remained that way from 1958 through 1966, with more than 50 percent of the earnings allocated for scholarships.[38]

During the early years of Ebony Fashion Fair, some designers refused to sell their garments to Mrs. Johnson, but she persisted. When it came to breaking down barriers at the couture houses in Paris, she did just that. As Norment states in her article, "Defining Fabulous: Celebrating 50 Years of the Ebony Fashion Fair," Mrs. Johnson was the only African American buyer as well as the largest buyer of couture fashions in the world. As Mrs. Johnson became well known in the fashion capitals, the designers began to look forward to visits from the stylish African American woman who often was accompanied by beautiful models.[39]

According to the "History" Web page:

A variety of nonprofit groups sponsors the show in each city, helping many organizations to raise money for charitable causes. Most often leading social and civic groups and sororities and fraternities have benefited from the show's efforts. The show is sponsored by nearly 180 nonprofit organizations with some cities alternating because of the travel time frame. . . . Today, hundreds of thousands of people attend the show each year.

Over 4,000 shows have been performed to date in the United States, the Caribbean, London, England, and Kingston, Jamaica. To date, Ebony Fashion Fair has raised more than $54 million for various scholarship groups, allowing hundreds of young people the opportunity to further their education.[40]

So what is the key for the longevity of Ebony Fashion Fair? Norment states that finding models that have a flair for fashion and innate sense of confidence—and using great music—has been key to Ebony Fashion Fair's longevity and why the show continues to be the leading force in presenting designer creations to the Black community. According to Staci R. Collins Jackson, assistant vice president at Johnson Publishing Company who oversees the operation of the Ebony Fashion Fair, the show still attracts sell-out crowds in venues across the country and the fact that "our younger attendees especially enjoy the R&B and hip hop music that we have infused into the show. . . . There is something for everyone, and that's why the show has staying power."[41]

Finally, my own personal experience covering the Ebony Fashion Fair event in Greensboro, North Carolina, with my wife in 2007 helped me to recognize more of the cultural impact that this event has with the local community as well as in other communities throughout the United States. Not only did the male and female models of varying physical sizes (slender, plus) put on an outstanding, entertaining fashion show, but they also provided the audience with very positive messages about ethnic and individual beauty as well as individual pride.

CONCLUSION

So what type of conclusions can we derive from this cultural-historical review of African American fashion? First and foremost, there is a wealth of untouched, cultural-historical information that can add to a deeper understanding of the reasons why African Americans feel strongly about fashion and why it is necessary for us to allow African Americans to define fashion for themselves. That's the major reason why this chapter highlighted the African American fashion versus European American mainstream society's fashion. Initially, one would not think that there needs to be this separation or discussion, yet after investigating the cultural-historical beginnings of fashion in the African American communities, one can easily see how social forces predicated more of a division between African American fashion versus European American mainstream society's fashion industry.

The fact that there are these two separate fashion show systems—the European American mainstream society's fashion and the Ebony Fashion Fair—indicates not only that American audiences and fashion designers prefer different types of fashion shows, but it also indicates that there is an underlying cultural preference for one type of fashion show versus another. Indeed, one would think that all fashion shows are alike. Yet when you attend a fashion show, like I experienced at the Ebony Fashion Fair show, there is an ethnic and cultural presence.

The ethnic presence was that a majority of the models were Americans of African descent. Secondly, all the models varied in skin color and build. Some women were slim, whereas others appeared to have more voluptuous shapes (hips and thighs). Third, they also had a plus size model. Finally, the male models were muscular-built and the same height.

The cultural presence was that the production included lively, up-tempo rhythm and blues and hip-hop music that the audience enjoyed as well. The familiarity of the music, stage show, and style of the presentation by the hostess made this fashion show distinctively African American.

These are the reasons why African Americans feel that they need to express their fashion style differently than mainstream European Americans. It allows African Americans to see themselves as part of the high-fashion show industry, and it also allows African Americans to make the decisions on the type of fashion that they prefer. What more can you ask?

CHAPTER 6

AFRICAN AMERICAN IMAGES AND THE ADVERTISING INDUSTRY

INTRODUCTION

Historically, the relationship between advertising and the use of African American images to sell or promote various products in America has always been a tenuous and sensitive topic. The fact that our physical images have and continue to be used in so many stereotypical settings suggest that European American mainstream society still doesn't totally understand the cultural impact that it has within African American communities throughout the United States.[1] In addition, even within the African American community and predominantly African American companies, they are also pressured to make sure that their physical images of African Americans match the agreed-upon physical images of the target African American population.

Dates and Barlow contend that racial images in the mass media are infused with color-coded positive and negative moralistic features.[2] Once these visual symbols become familiar and accepted, they fuel misperceptions, perpetuate misunderstandings, or correct misperceptions and perpetuate a greater understanding among the races. Thus racial representations help to mold public opinion, then hold it in place and set the agenda for public discussion on the race issue in the media and in the society at large.

In the case of African Americans, stereotypes are especially effective at conveying ideological messages because they are so laden with ritual and myth. Stereotypical black images most often are frozen, incapable of growth, change, innovation, or transformation. That's why the physical images of African Americans in the early history of America are still with

us today (i.e., Aunt Jemima, Sambo) and continue to perpetuate misunderstandings as to the *physical diversity* and *physical reality* within the African
American population.[3]

As Adorno stated about the impact of stereotypes on the psyche of
American culture:

The more stereotypes become reified and rigid in the present setup of the culture industries, the less people are likely to change their preconceived ideals with the progress of
experience. The more opaque and complicated modern life becomes, the more people
are tempted to cling desperately to clichés which seem to bring some order into the otherwise understandable.[4]

This reveals the attitude that, to use one of the advertising catch
phrases of the Canon camera company several years ago, "Image is
Everything." This is true particularly when using physical images of
African Americans to sell a product as well as to advertise to the African
American population.

As this chapter focuses upon advertising, let us begin with a general definition. Advertising is defined as "the action of attracting public attention
to a product or business."[5] Ever since the beginning of advertising, three
rules have prevailed:

To advertise to people ready, willing, and able to buy;
To use the media that reach them; and
To make advertisements that would win their business.[6]

As for the African American consumer, we want not only to be
courted for our money as others are but also we respond to the respect
implicit in the courting process, when the advertisement is neither
patronizing nor condescending. Dates and Barlow reported that former
state Georgia Senator Julian Bond in the 1970s and 1980s said the following about the African American consumer: "We want to believe that
we are buying the best of the line, the top ticket item . . . that the company that sells to us also hires us and has us on its board . . . that our
pictures will be in some of the ads without the use of patronizing, spe-
cious street jargon."[7]

Although it took much longer than expected and desired by most
African Americans, European American mainstream society has been significantly improving their advertising strategies to the African American
consumer market. From $77 billion earnings in the mid 1970s to more
than $140 billion in the mid 1980s and to over $200 billion in the 1990s,
European American mainstream society has finally realized that effective
advertising and marketing to the African American market can definitely
result in major profit earnings for any company.[8]

In fact, here are some of the latest advertising data collected on the U.S. African American population with regards to spending pattern:

- African Americans account for more than 30% of industry spending in the $4 billion hair market.
- Among African American households, 63% purchased used vehicles, and 37% purchased new vehicles.
- African American consumers spend more on telephone services than any other consumer group. Their expenditures in this category total $918 annually, or 8.1% more than the average consumer.
- Within the entertainment category, African American consumers allocate nearly twice as much money than the average U.S. consumer to purchase televisions, radios, and sound equipment (59.6% vs. 32.2%).
- According to ethnic the marketing director at Kraft Foods, the average African American family spends 30% more on weekly groceries than the U.S. population at large.[9]

In addition to this data on African Americans' spending patterns, the Magazine Publishers of America report titled "African American Market Profile" states that African Americans are more likely than the average U.S. consumer to:

- Place a high premium on the status of owning tangible items;
- Spend more for what is perceived as "the best"—64% vs 51% of European Americans;
- Want to dress in the latest fashions in order to enhance appearance;
- Be brand loyal and rely upon certain brands to help them make informed purchase decisions [10]

With this type of data on the spending patterns of African Americans, corporate America recognizes that the African American market has and will continue to play a critical role in American culture. There is no doubt that this market will continue to increase in the future, and corporate America is making a much more sincere, direct, and culturally competent approach in reaching the African American market.

POSITIVE AFRICAN AMERICAN IMAGES WITH
NEW ADVERTISING CAMPAIGNS

Without a doubt, over the centuries, decades, and years, a very large percentage of the advertising campaigns in America did not respect or correctly use African American images with their particular products.[11] Even in 2007, there are still a wide array of misrepresentations or stereotypical images of African Americans with certain national and local advertising campaigns.

Nonetheless, there are a vast number of national advertising campaigns that not only show African Americans in positive images, but they also show African Americans in all of their physical diversity, as opposed to only showing a certain physical type. For example, take a look at your daily or weekly newspaper and check out the national advertisement pamphlets and flyers. What do you notice? On one level, you notice that there are more persons of color advertising products. Products ranging from foods, clothing, sportswear, fitness apparel, toys, appliances, furniture, automobiles, and outdoor patio furniture. You name the item, there is most likely a person of color advertising it. Yet look closer; do you notice anything else?

More than likely, the African American who is advertising the product looks physically fit, showing more well-rounded hips, thighs, and butt, as well as muscular physical attributes. Whether the African American models are women, men, adolescents, or children, all of them reflect the healthy, physical diversity of the African American population. This is a definite change from either the extra-thin to the extra-heavy African American models that often became associated with national advertising campaigns.

For example, advertisements from companies such as Sears, JC Penney, Circuit City, K-Mart, Target, and even Home Depot all show African American models who are not only physically fit but also well-proportioned and shapely. The JC Penney and the Home Depot ads are particularly noteworthy because they strategically highlight the African American woman's distinguishable, curvy hips. In fact in the Home Depot ad,[12] it shows a professional African American woman wearing a fitting slack outfit, standing in a modern kitchen with her cell phone in one hand and the other hand on a laptop computer while the new modern washer is operating next to her.

The physical symbolism of this advertisement implies that professional African American women not only live like this African American woman model, that is, as a business professional, but they also maintain their healthy, shapely bodies. That is the difference in the new advertisements today. American mainstream culture, particularly American corporate culture, has embraced and is attempting to promote a greater appreciation of the healthy, physical diversity and body types associated with the African American population today!

POSITIVE ADVERTISING CAMPAIGNS AND AFRICAN AMERICAN CELEBRITIES

In the business world, it has been quite routine for advertisers to use celebrities to promote and sell products. In the 1970s, the advertising industry began to use African Americans as star presenters on television and in print ads.[13] During this period, African American entertainer Lola

Falana advertised "Tigris" perfume, while Bill Cosby began to pitch for the Del Monte Corporation. Cosby did an unidentified voice-over, using his gentle, whimsical humor to make the product name heard and remembered and to make the commercial palatable. The General Foods Corporation began using Cosby as a spokesman for Jell-O in 1973, and in 1976 he began appearing as a star presenter for the Ford Motor Company.

According to Dates and Barlow, Cosby was chosen by these companies because research had proven that he exuded an unusual amount of believability and warmth. Thus, he could help each company in its campaign to build a youthful, warm, and modern image as it positioned itself in the market.[14]

The 1980s saw a proliferation of African American talent in the forefront as star presenters in advertisements. In addition to Bill Cosby, Dates and Barlow note that the recording industry's Michael Jackson and Lionel Richie appeared for Pepsi-Cola and Whitney Houston for Diet Coke. Bubba Smith, a former defensive lineman for the Baltimore Colts, Oakland Raiders, and Houston Oilers promoted Miller Lite Beer, and William "The Refrigerator" Perry, a tackle for the Chicago Bears, endorsed McDonald's hamburgers. Herschel Walker was selling Big Macs and Adidas sneakers; Julius Erving (Dr. J.) was pitching Crest toothpaste and Converse basketball shoes; and Reggie Jackson was selling Pentax cameras, Panasonic video equipment, and Nabisco cereals.[15] In addition, Michael Jordan, former NBA Chicago Bulls and Washington Wizards basketball player and minor league baseball player, advertised just about everything, but was best known for his special Nike (Air Jordan) shoes. Thus it becomes quite apparent that celebrity African Americans have had crossover appeal in promoting a wide variety of products to American mainstream audiences and African American audiences for a number of years.

Currently, the advertising industry has continued its incorporation of African American celebrities to advertise and promote their products to specific ethnic and American mainstream markets. The use of a trusted and well-respected African American celebrity for any advertising campaign provides the company with a direct connection of their product to not only a specific ethnic market (African American) but also to the American mainstream market.

UNSTEREOTYPICAL FEMALE AFRICAN AMERICAN CELEBRITIES

This part of the chapter highlights four major African American celebrities who have created and established their cross market appeal in the African American market and American mainstream market. They are also individuals who are quite comfortable and proud of their body image and full-figured body type that happens to be counter to the standard body type and image associated with European American mainstream society. These individuals are:

- **Mo'Nique**—an African American comedienne, television host, and entrepreneur
- **Raven Symone**—an African American actress, entertainer and entrepreneur
- **Queen Latifah**—an African American actress, singer, entertainer and entrepreneur
- **Oprah Winfrey**—an African American television host and corporate entrepreneur.

Mo'Nique

Born Monique Imes and now known as "Mo'Nique," this actress and no-nonsense comedienne is skyrocketing to worldwide fame. In a recent *Ebony* magazine article, Mo'Nique says that growing up in Baltimore, Maryland, she was inspired by her grandmother and Oprah Winfrey, who was a local television anchor at the time. This was the time period in which she gained confidence in her appearance and her abilities.

Mo'Nique reached one-name fame after playing Nikki Parker on the UPN series, *The Parkers*. She won two NAACP Image Awards for Outstanding Lead Actress in a Comedy Series, and made history as the first female to host *It's Showtime at the Apollo*. Her 2003 New York Times best selling book, *Skinny Women are Evil*, rallied big women everywhere to embrace their full bodies. Additionally, her new television show, *Mo'Nique's F.A.T. Chance* ("Fabulous and Thick"), a popular Oxygen cable reality series, showcases full-figured women.

In fact, *Mo'Nique* and ten of her *F.A.T. Chance* contestants went to Paris, and while there, they decided to flaunt their birthday suits (in an artist studio) that were stylishly accessorized with a little body paint. *Mo'Nique* said, "For big women, our biggest fear is exposing our bodies. Women are starting to love themselves for themselves."[16]

Raven Symone

Born Raven-Symone Christina Pearman and now known as Raven or Raven Symone, this young actress, rhythm and blues and pop singer, songwriter, dancer, and television producer is already a veteran of the entertainment and advertising industries at the age of twenty-three. As an infant, Raven worked for Atlanta's Young Faces, Inc., Modeling Agency and was featured in local print advertisements.

At age two, she worked with Ford Models, Inc., in New York City and appeared in ads for Ritz Crackers, Jell-O, Fisher-Price, and Cool Whip.

A few years later, she landed the role on the *Cosby Show* and played the character Olivia for three years. After the *Cosby Show,* Raven Symone starred in her own series *That's So Raven*—a Disney Channel Original Series that became an overnight success. This show has grossed over $400 million dollars and easily became the most successful show on the Disney Channel.[17]

Yet with all of her success, Raven Symone does not fit the physical image of the typical young Hollywood actress/entertainer. When asked if her voluptuous figure ever stands in the way of getting work, she responds: "I sometimes think it does. I'm not a size 2 and I am tan! "But I don't let that bother me."[18]

Queen Latifah

Born Dana Elaine Owens and now known as Queen Latifah, this American rapper, jazz singer, actress, producer, entrepreneur, restaurateur, and philanthropist has conquered several industries, especially the entertainment and fashion industries. Beginning with her first rap album, *All Hail the Queen,* in 1989 to her latest album in 2007, Queen Latifah has earned a Grammy Award and five additional Grammy nominations associated with her music.[19]

As for her acting career, Queen Latifah starred in the hit television series *Living Single* (1993–1998), had her own talk show, *The Queen Latifah Show* (1999–2001), and appeared in major motion pictures. The movie role that catapulted Latifah to international movie fame was the movie *Chicago,* for which she earned an Academy Award nomination.[20]

Yet for millions of women across the country and around the globe, Queen Latifah is the queen of the full-figured beauties and a role model and inspiration for the ordinary women. Latifah has been a celebrity spokesperson for Cover Girl cosmetics (2001), Curvation ladies underwear, and now a new upscale clothing line called Dana O.

In a recent *Ebony* magazine article, Queen Latifah says her concept for the Dana O collection is based upon beautiful materials and excellent cuts for the full figured woman's body. Furthermore, Latifah says:

For too long, people have devalued this so-called plus size market. There are 65 million of us in America. For a long time, everything that was made for us was just big sheets of materials, boxy and wrong cuts. We have curves. We have a figure. Things need to be tailored more to our body types.[21]

The impact of Queen Latifah's clothing wear along with her Cover Girl cosmetics line provides companies such as Procter and Gamble a great opportunity to promote more of the positive physical images associated with African American women. In fact, Queen Latifah is also a national spokesperson for Procter and Gamble's new "My Black is Beautiful" campaign, which is aimed at celebrating the beauty of African American women in all their various sizes, shapes, and shades. For example, Esi Eggleston Bracey, vice president and general manager of North America and Global Cosmetics said the following about Queen Latifah: "Queen Latifah is an untraditional but clearly aspirational beauty. She defies stereotypes, and women all over the country resonate with her—regardless of age, ethnicity, or size."[22]

Oprah Winfrey

Born Oprah Gail Winfrey, this full-figured talk show host is

the American multiple-Emmy Award winning host of *The Oprah Winfrey Show*, the highest-rated talk show in television history. She is also an influential book critic, an Academy Award-nominated actress, and a magazine publisher. She has been ranked the richest African American of the twentieth century, the most philanthropic African American of all time, and the world's only black billionaire for three straight years. She is also. . . the most influential woman in the world.[23]

Yet before Oprah became the Oprah the world knows now, she was a news anchor in Nashville, Tennessee, and in Baltimore, Maryland, by 1976. According to *Fortune Magazine,* in her first major television job in Baltimore, the station bosses wanted her to change her hair, lips, nose, and just about everything else.[24]

Dennis Swanson, who recruited her to Chicago in 1983, was the first executive who let Oprah be Oprah! He recalls:

I hadn't met her before she came to my office. She desperately wanted to be hired to do the *AM Chicago* show. She said, "Do you have any concerns about me?"
   I said, "No, not that I can think of."
   "Well, you know I'm black," she said.
   I told her, "Yeah, I figured that out."
   Then she said, "You know I'm overweight,"
   I said, "So am I. I don't want you to change your appearance."[25]

According to *Fortune Magazine,* it was Dennis Swanson who convinced Oprah that she could succeed by being herself. Within a couple of years, Oprah's show went national, and the rest is history!

In addition to *The Oprah Winfrey Show*, Oprah's company, Harpo, Inc., owns *Harpo Films* and *O! The Oprah Magazine*. Ironically, one of the biggest successes for Oprah Winfrey has been the launch of her magazine. After the second year of operating, *O!* raked in more than $140 million in revenues and became the most successful startup magazine in the industry.[26]

The magazine reaches a richer set of fans than those watching the daytime television show. It is designed to give confident, smart women the tools they need to explore and reach for their dreams, to express their individual style, and to make choices that will lead to a happier and more fulfilling life. With Oprah inspiring the editorial content, *O!* serves as a catalyst for transforming women's lives.

Additionally, with lush photography gracing oversized pages, each issue offers compelling stories and empowering ideas stamped with Oprah's unique vision on such topics as:

- Health and fitness;
- Relationship and self-discovery;
- 'Book That Made a Difference;'
- 'Phenomenal Women'—profiles, inspired by the Maya Angelou poem, of women who overcome adversity in their lives to realize their potential;
- 'What I Know for Sure'—a column about personal belief systems; and
- Beauty, fashion, and home design.

Interestingly, what really sells Oprah's magazine is the monthly front cover. The monthly front cover features the one and only Oprah Winfrey—photographed in a stylized manner that shows her up close, wearing the latest fashions from the hottest designers, and looking simply beautiful! Each month, Oprah showcases her full-figured body and face so that the world can see another aspect of physical diversity and beauty from an African American woman. This is the true impact of the *O! The Oprah Magazine.* Oprah's image on the front cover challenges the perpetual misconceptions and stereotypes of beauty and healthy, physical diversity associated with African American women and all women in American mainstream society.

CONCLUSION

It should be quite apparent to the average consumer today that the advertising industry has dramatically changed their strategies in marketing their products to specific ethnic and mainstream markets more than ever before. At one time, the advertising industry did not believe it was necessary to change their approach in marketing to the specific ethnic markets such as the African American market. Yet over time, the industry realized that, in order to be successful and to generate the interest and respect for their products, they had to develop a more genuine and culturally competent advertising strategy for the African American market.

The advertising industry also realized through market research that the African American market spends a lot of disposable income on a wide variety of household, entertainment, lifestyle, hair, beauty, fitness, and fashion products. In order to continue to have a bigger market share profit of the African American market, the advertising industry has reinvented their approach and is making a sincere cultural effort to connect with the growing African American market.

In the years to come, do not be surprised to see more persons of color advertising a wider variety of products. Advertisers are always conceiving new approaches to reach new, untapped markets. The African American market is still that untapped market.

—— CHAPTER 7 ——

AFRICAN AMERICAN BODY IMAGES AND THE FITNESS INDUSTRY

INTRODUCTION

Perhaps one of the biggest problems that I have witnessed over the past five to ten years is the health and fitness industry's almost total neglect of the African American population. It has been a very disturbing trend that continues to grow each and every year, and no one appears to be doing anything about it or feels like that it is worth marketing health and fitness products and services to the African American market. Not only are few books, magazines, or videos targeted at African Americans for health and fitness, but also very few physically fit body images of African Americans are connected to health and fitness programs. Sure, there are the professional athletes and professional training books, magazines, or videos, but absolutely nothing showing the average African American attempting to get into shape.

If you think that I'm imagining this blatant neglect of health and fitness to the African American population, do your own experiment! Simply go to your local grocery store or bookstore and visit the magazine rack displays. What do you see? I'm sorry that is not the right question. *What do you NOT see at the magazine racks or book shelves?* That's right, you do not see very many magazines or books showing physically fit African Americans on the front cover. How does the health and fitness industry get away with this blatant neglect of the African American market when in fact we have so many professional athletes in the country?

What has been even more disturbing is the fact that European American mainstream society feels that we do not even care about our health and fitness. Nothing can be farther from the truth, because research shows that African Americans do care about their health and fitness—it's just that we view and conduct exercise and fitness differently than European American mainstream society.

For example, in a study titled "African American Women's Experiences with Physical Activity in Their Daily Lives," researchers conducted focus groups among women aged 35–50 years, healthy, employed and unemployed, middle- to low-income urban dwellers. The focus groups were led by an African American nurse, and other key African American facilitators were involved in the study.

The major facilitator themes that emerged during analysis for African American women included:

- daily routine,
- practical and convenient activities,
- personal safety,
- child care
- weight loss,
- stress reduction,
- knowledge and commitment,
- enjoyment,
- presence of pet,
- family and peer support,
- home and work facilities, and
- daylight and climate conditions.

Some of the comments from the African American women are as follows:

We like the idea of exercising (together) and we knew that there was going to be more than one person there so that's a group environment. I went (to exercise class) religiously because there were people there.

When the weather is nice, I can leave my house and go to the fairgrounds and I walk about two miles . . . and we do that about every day we have enough daylight. You can walk three miles before you know it, and you really feel good . . . you feel like you can do anything.[1]

The major barriers, however, that emerged during analysis for African American women included: (a) lack of child care, (b) no person to exercise with, (c) competing responsibilities, (d) lack of space in the home, (e) inability to use exercise facilities at work, (f) lack of understanding and motivation, (g) fatigue, and (h) unsafe neighborhoods.[2] Therefore, this study suggests that African American women do care about fitness and exercise; they just view it differently, and it has to fit within their lifestyles and cultural preferences associated with fitness exercise.

Because verifiable evidence from a wide variety of studies shows this apparent difference in preference and pattern for exercise and fitness programs for African Americans, why does the fitness industry not attempt to reach the

African American population in the way that we prefer? Additionally, why is there such a disconnect with European American mainstream society's magazines' and books' ability to show physically fit, positive body images of African Americans on the front cover of their magazines and books?

The answers to these two previous questions are simple. First, the major reasons why the fitness industry has not attempted overwhelmingly to market their health and fitness products to the African American population is because they believe the African American market would not generate as much revenue as other niche markets.

Advertising executives also believe that the African American population does not want to purchase health and fitness products with their disposable income.[2] Unfortunately, both of these reasons are primarily based upon misperceptions and misconceptions associated with the African American population. The fact is simply that African Americans are more than willing to spend their disposable income on health and fitness products as long as these products are marketed to them in a culturally competent and respectful way.

Second, the major reason why there is a major disconnect with European American mainstream society's magazines' and books' inability to show physically fit, positive body images of African Americans on the front covers is because they believed that American mainstream society would not accept a physically fit African American body type on a cover of a mainstream magazine or book. Again, this reason is based upon misperception and lack of understanding of the American mainstream market.

Nonetheless, a new health and fitness trend is emerging in the fitness industry, and it directly involves African Americans. This chapter will highlight several examples of an emerging trend that shows not only are African Americans being included into American mainstream society's health and fitness programs, but we are also becoming the role models for the new health and fitness trends as they relate to physical fitness and preferred body types. What is particularly amazing about this emerging trend is that the fitness industry finally recognizes that African Americans are involved in a wide array of high-level, professional fitness programs and sports (i.e., football, baseball, basketball, track and field, soccer, tennis, and golf) and the fact that many of the best athletes in each of these sports are African Americans. Therefore, it makes very good business sense for the fitness industry to feature a prominent African American athlete or an African American model in their advertisements and promotions.

NEW AMERICAN MAINSTREAM HEALTH
AND FITNESS BOOKS

Recently, a number of high-performance fitness training books have featured African Americans on the front cover. For example, the front cover of the book *Training for Speed, Agility, and Quickness* portrays a physically fit, athletic African American woman training on a track field. This book describes the drills and workouts that individuals need to get a step ahead of the competition, and it also allows readers to see, through illustrations, exactly how to perform key tests and execute the best and most complex drills. Sample training programs are included for sports such as baseball, softball, basketball, soccer, field hockey, volleyball, football, tennis, netball, cricket, rugby, and Australian rules football.[3]

Functional Training for Sports features a muscular, physically fit African American man in a fitness training room on the front cover. This book guides the reader through a complete system that focuses on training one's body the way it will be used during competition to develop movement skills, body positions, and explosive power essential for all sports. The book provides tests that allow individuals to assess their strengths and determine where they need to start in the progression. The progression focuses on training the torso, the upper body, and the lower body.[4]

The cover of *Muscle Mechanics* highlights a muscular, physically fit African American man, with biceps showing, lifting a barbell. This book teaches the reader how to train for strength, definition, and muscle size using sixty-five of the most effective exercises covering all the major muscle groups. By combining full-color anatomical illustrations and expert technical guidance, this book helps the individual to better understand how to properly target specific muscles by using the most efficient alignment, positioning, and lifting technique for each exercise. *Muscle Mechanics* also highlights three programs for base strength, full-body fitness, and advanced split routines, showing how to combine the exercises into progressive strength programs.[5]

Finally, the book that completely captured and fascinated the American mainstream health and fitness audience in 2006 was *L.A. Shape Diet: The 14-Day Total Weight Loss Plan*. This book was one of the biggest selling diet and fitness books in all of the major book retail stores for two years. (www.amazon.com/L-Shape-Diet-14-Day-Weight/dp/006073787) What was most surprising about this book was that it pictured a shapely African American woman wearing only a white bikini bottom on the front cover; she is sitting on a diving board with her back to the audience. This visual image of the African American woman's body symbolized how an individual's body could look if she followed the new L.A. Diet plan.[6]

Dr. David Herber, Director of the UCLA Center for Human Nutrition, specifically wrote the *L.A. Shape Diet* book to encourage women and men to lose the desired weight, while also recognizing that everyone has a certain body shape. From the inside fly of the dust jacket: "Dr. Herber maintains that everyone is born with a particular shape, and this shape makes a huge difference in how an individual should approach weight loss. He teaches the difference between the shape you can change and the shape you cannot."[7] Specifically, Dr. Herber states:

Shape is less of an obsession with men, but they also need to be realistic about their potential best body shape. There are no best shapes other than the one you achieve personally—and you can achieve it, no matter where you are starting from. The key is to be happy with who you are and to embrace and love your best shape.[8]

Apparently, the remarks from Dr. Herber and his *L.A. Shape Diet* book indicated that he thought his diet was exactly the type of diet and weight-loss program that many mainstream Americans were waiting for.

What is most fascinating about this emerging trend in the health and fitness industry to showcase physically fit African American body types on mainstream American health and fitness books is that mainstream America is accepting and embracing these physical images of African Americans. Just a few years ago, these physical images of African Americans were primarily marketed strictly to the African American population, yet now these physical images have crossed over to mainstream America. This is truly an indicator that a cultural revolution toward greater acceptance of varying African American body images and body types as the standard for physical fitness and athletic fitness training has occurred in our society.

AMERICAN MAINSTREAM HEALTH AND FITNESS CLUBS

Some of the places where you can see the positive portrayal of African American physical images is at the national health and fitness clubs. Although it was a mystery as to why African Americans were not included in the initial marketing of the health and fitness clubs, currently they are making considerable effort for inclusion of African Americans on all their major marketing strategies targeted to the general public.

For example, Curves is the world's largest fitness franchise and the tenth largest franchise chain in the world. With 10,000 locations in more than fifty-five countries, Curves has made exercise available to over four million women around the world, many of whom are in the gym for the first time.

Currently, the Curves Web site (www.curves.com) features all different types of women, especially full-figured, physically fit, African American women. Created by a European American husband and wife team, this new thirty-minute fitness concept combines strength training and sustained cardiovascular activity through safe and effective hydraulic resistance. The comfortable, supportive environment was designed for women, and it was immediately successful.[9]

Another major national health and fitness club that is finally marketing to the African American market is Bally Total Fitness. Advertised as the largest, most experienced health club chain in North America, Bally Total Fitness has approximately 400 locations in 70 U.S. cities and 3.5 million members. Bally recently opened fitness clubs in South Korea, China, and the Bahamas as well.

The mission of Bally Total Fitness is to improve the health and quality of life for people through personalized, accessible wellness programs. Not only has Bally Total Fitness included more physically fit African Americans in their television and Web site commercials, but they also have included specific group exercise classes such as Funk, Hip Hop, and Salsa to appeal directly to the African American market.[10]

Another health and fitness club, 24-Hour Fitness, has attempted to make fitness a way of life for everyone, including African Americans. Advertised as the world's largest privately owned and operated fitness center chain, 24-Hour Fitness has grown to more than 370 clubs in 16 states and boasts more than 3 million members.

In 2000, 24-Hour Fitness partnered with five athletes, two of whom are African Americans—NBA basketball legend Earvin "Magic" Johnson and current NBA star Shaquille O'Neal. Specifically, the partnership with Shaquille O'Neal helped to create the new 24-Hour Fitness Shaq Sport Clubs—a fitness club with Shaq-sized amenities in the clubs and locker rooms.

Interestingly, the partnership with Shaquille O'Neal started after Shaq spent the 2003 off-season with a certified personal trainer from 24-Hour Fitness. Impressed with the results and the company, Shaq signed on to create a chain of uniquely branded clubs to be a new face for 24-Hour Fitness print and television advertising. Thus the partnership with an NBA basketball player such as Shaquille O'Neal has helped 24-Hour Fitness capture more of the African American market as well as other markets, because Shaq has a tremendous crossover appeal to a wide variety of markets.

Finally, a national health and fitness program (not a club)—Billy Blanks Taebo—features the African American founder, Billy Blanks, teaching millions of people around the world how to get into shape and feel good about their health. Billy Blanks Taebo is a program that combines the best of a variety of different exercise disciplines to provide an overall workout. It combines the self-awareness and control of martial arts, the focus and strength of boxing, and the grace and rhythm of dance. Most importantly, Taebo is an exercise routine that teaches people how to communicate with their bodies and how the mind should operate with the spirit.[11]

What is most fascinating about the phenomenal success of Billy Blanks Taebo is that he has branded himself as a revolutionary total body fitness guru. He is in demand to not only teach his Taebo fitness classes to thousands of followers, but he has also been most successful in marketing his program to mainstream America. In fact, his most loyal base of followers is European American women. Thus, Billy Blanks' positive physically fit image helps to sell and motivate millions of people around the world to purchase his fitness training products and to become physically fit as well.

AFRICAN AMERICAN HEALTH AND FITNESS BOOKS

Although there have been a number of African American health and fitness books published over the years, the past few years have seen somewhat of a resurgence in health and fitness books designed specifically for African Americans. *Slim Down Sister*, the first weight-loss book written especially for African American women, addresses the serious health concerns facing African American women today and offers a comprehensive, get-down-to-it program of diet and exercise that empowers sisters to take control of their weight and health.[12] Here are the key points to this ground-breaking book:

- Why losing weight is more difficult for black women;
- The critical role that African American traditions and culture play in contributing to obesity;
- The Soul-Food Pyramid—how to cook up the foods you love without all the health-jeopardizing fat and calories; and
- Specific exercises designed for your body type.[13]

Slim Down Sister is one of those books that truly engages the African American woman in a style, dialogue, and approach that makes it so much easier for any African American woman, regardless of background, to take action about her weight, fitness, and exercise situation. We need more books like this one.

The other book that I want to highlight in this section is MaDonna Grimes' *Work It Out: The Black Women's Guide to Getting the Body You Always Wanted*. Fitness expert MaDonna Grimes offers African American women a different ideal to work toward—one suited for their unique physiques. Drawing from her experience as a professional dancer, choreographer, fitness competitor, and winner of Miss Fitness America and Miss Fitness International competitions, Grimes has fashioned a fitness program specifically for African American women, to help them attain their fitness goals and build self-esteem.[14]

Grimes states the major reason why she wrote her book:

I just got tired of watching women with beautiful shapely curves hold themselves up to impossible ideals and try to redesign their bodies into shapes that they were just never meant to be, leaving them like failures in the end. You know how good you can look. Enhance your curves; don't lose them.[15]

Grimes offers a simple plan to allow the individual to be consistent when it comes to building and maintaining his or her body. Her integration of dance and weight training along with dieting is designed to transform the body and also to provide permanent weight loss.[16] She states:

The first step of your weight training is, believe it or not, cardio. You've got to engage in twenty to thirty minutes of some kind of cardio exercise to warm up your muscles. You can go with either the treadmill or the stationary bike; both will burn calories while elevating your heart rate to its target range. Personally, I love doing my cardio on a treadmill. It works you harder than the bike. You can incline the treadmill to make it even more challenging. And, of course, you get all the same electronic programs for motivation that go with the stationary bike.[17]

Grimes further states that step two of the weight-training program is the actual weight training.

I'm telling you that this workout should not last more than thirty minutes. What's the point of wasting precious time? I want you in and out of the gym with the best possible outcome for your time invested. Unless I say otherwise for a specific exercise, start with the minimum comfortable weight, and over time as it gets easier to lift that weight, work your way up in 10-pound increments.[18]

Surprisingly, *Work It Out* is one of the first health and fitness books designed specifically for African American women by an African American woman fitness expert. Grimes completes this groundbreaking book with the following parting message: "Sisters are doing it themselves. But we still have to keep the faith and live the life that brings emotional well-being, spiritual fulfillment, and a healthy, sexy body to be proud of."[19]

AFRICAN AMERICAN ATHLETES AND FITNESS

From the early beginnings of professional sports in America to the present, African American athletes have excelled and often become the best when given an opportunity to compete at that sport. From early world-class athletes such as Jesse Owens, Jackie Robinson, Jack Johnson, Althea Gibson, Arthur Ashe, Wilma Rudolph, Hank Aaron, Willie Mays, Bill Russell, Oscar Robinson, Wilt Chamberlain, and Muhammad Ali to the contemporary athletes such as Venus Williams, Serena Williams, Tiger Woods, and thousands of other professional athletes in football, baseball, basketball, boxing, track and field, tennis, and golf, African Americans have displayed world-class fitness and athletic ability throughout the entire history of organized professional sport.

To highlight the high level of physical fitness and positive body images among today's African American athletes, this section focuses upon three athletes: Venus Williams, her younger sister Serena Williams (tennis superstars), and Tiger Woods (golf superstar). The primary purpose of recognizing these athletes is to show how they are not only exceptional, physically fit African American athletes, but how they have also been totally embraced and promoted by mainstream corporate America because of their crossover market appeal.

Venus Williams

American Venus Ebone Starr Williams has been ranked the world's number one female tennis player. As of July 2007, she was the reigning Wimbledon ladies' singles champion.

Venus Williams's record speaks for itself. Williams has won the Olympic gold medal in women's tennis and fourteen Grand Slam titles, including six singles (four at Wimbledon), six women's doubles, and two mixed double titles.[20]

Venus Williams is also a businesswoman and CEO of her interior design firm, V Starr Interiors. Williams's company garnered prominence by designing the set of a PBS talk show; the company also designed the Olympic athletes apartments as a part of the U.S. bid package for New York to host the 2012 games, and residences and businesses in the Palm Beach, Florida, area. Ms. Williams has received substantial endorsement deals, including one with Reebok shoes for $40 million. She also recently teamed up with a major mainstream retailer, Steve and Barry's, to launch her own fashion line, EleVen.[21]

Venus says this about her fashion line:

I love fashion and the idea that I am using my design education to actually create clothing and footwear that I will wear on and off the tennis court is a dream come true for me.

The vision has been to create a collection that will allow women to enjoy an active lifestyle while remaining fashionable at the same time. I'm thrilled with everything we've created to launch EleVen.[22]

Officially launched in November 2007, Venus Williams's EleVen has quickly become a major success, primarily because the clothes, shoes, and accessories are economically priced, and the clothing line fits a wide variety of body types. Ironically, I was able to find out more about Venus William's EleVen fashion line through my own fieldwork and by observing the reaction from my wife and daughter after they had purchased a couple of EleVen outfits.

According to my informants (my wife and my daughter), the EleVen clothing line is comfortable, form-fitting, stylish, and economical. The outfits are designed for teenagers and women of all ages who live an active lifestyle. An entire outfit, including athletic shoes, did not cost more than $60.00! Specifically, my informants said the following after they modeled their individual outfits: "Finally, an active wear that fits my body, and I feel good in it."

Serena Williams

Serena Jameka Williams is also a former world number one ranked female tennis player who has won eight Grand Slam single titles, twenty-eight career titles, and an Olympic gold medal in women's doubles. She is the last player, male or female, to have held all four Grand Slams at the same time.[23]

Serena's playing style is described as being very fast around the court. Her athleticism and her physical strength give her the ability to hit the ball efficiently from very difficult positions. Her physical strength is intimidating. To build her massive arms, she regularly exercises with one arm on weights that most people would struggle to lift with both arms. Because of her physicality, she is capable of overpowering her opponents when returning serves.[24]

In an interview with *Savoy* magazine, Serena was asked about whether she experienced racism in tennis. Serena responded:

Well, we've only been out of slavery for a little over a hundred years. So obviously you can't go anywhere and say there is no racism. Now, because of who we [Venus and I] are and because of what we've accomplished, I don't experience it as much anymore. But I'm sure it's there.[25]

Finally, as her sister Venus did, Serena developed her own line of designer clothing called Aneres. She has modeled her designs and plans to sell her clothing in boutiques in Miami and Los Angeles.

Tiger Woods

Eldrick Tiger Woods is an American professional golfer whose achievements to date rank him among the most successful golfers of all time. In 2006, Tiger Woods was the highest paid professional athlete, having earned an estimated $100 million from winnings and endorsements. At the end of the 2007 season, Tiger Woods was on top of the golf world again, winning the PGA Championship (http://sports.espn.go.com/golf/pgachampionship07/news/story?id=2971556).

Woods has won thirteen professional major golf championships, second among all male players of all time, and sixty-one PGA Tour events, fifth all time. He has more career major wins and career PGA Tour wins than any other active golfer. He is the youngest player to achieve the Career Grand Slam, and the youngest and fastest to win fifty tournaments on Tour. He has been awarded PGA Player of the Year a record nine times, tied Jack Nicklaus's record of leading the money list in eight different seasons, and has been named Associated Press Male Athlete of the Year four times.[26]

Tiger Woods's golf playing style has been characterized as powerful, hitting and driving the golf ball longer distances than his competitors. In fact, Tiger is largely responsible for a shift to higher standards of athleticism among professional golfers because of his daily workout and physical regimen. He is also known for putting in more hours of practice than most.[27]

Tiger Woods has also been called the most marketable athlete in the world. Shortly after his twenty-first birthday in 1996, Woods began signing numerous endorsement deals with companies, including General Motors, Titleist, General Mills, American Express, Accenture, and Nike. In 2000, Woods signed a five-year, $105 million contract extension with Nike. It was the largest endorsement deal ever signed by an athlete at that time.[28]

Tiger's additional endorsement deals include Buick and their Enclave luxury SUVs, Tiger Woods PGA Tour series of video games, Gillette Champions razor, and a new Gatorade sports drink. The new Gatorade sports drink called "Gatorade Tiger" marks Woods's first U.S. deal with a beverage company and his first licensing agreement.[29]

With all his accomplishments, Tiger Woods readily acknowledges that his golfing skills and training are all due to the very early training from his father, Earl Woods, as well as the spiritual and mental support from his mother, Kultida. Interestingly, in Earl Woods's book, *Training a Tiger,* he had stated the following about his son:

Mindful of golf's mushrooming popularity, the unimaginable good fortune this game has brought to him, and the need to reach out to others, Tiger has envisioned the establishment of a personal charitable foundation through which he can funnel some of the fruits of his labor to those in need. Initially, this foundation will address the problem of the self-image of our youth through the use of sports psychology techniques. Self-worth is a critical prerequisite for success. If Tiger can help to instill in countless other aspiring athletes the sense of pride and purpose that he has gleaned from his family and golf experiences, then he will have made a difference in the world that transcends tournaments and fame. For the true sweetness of victory lies not in simply savoring your own accomplishment but in passing the baton to give someone else the same opportunity.[30]

CONCLUSION

Apparently, the crossover appeal of phenomenal athletes such as Tiger Woods, Serena Williams, Venus Williams, and so many other African American athletes has shown the fitness industry that a much larger percentage of the African American population than originally perceived function as role models for today's type of high-performance physical fitness. Examples of African American high-level performance physical fitness are seen every day in all the professional sports.

For instance, the training sports apparel company Under Armour, which markets training gear for all the major competitive sports, recently became even more successful in 2006 and 2007 because of their marketing campaign featuring physically fit, professional football players.[31] Vernon Davis, tight end for the San Francisco 49ers, received the most attention and helped launch their new training sports footwear. "Click-Clack," as the new advertising commercial was called, featured Vernon Davis as well as other NFL professional football players going through their fitness training workout using the new Under Armour footwear. "If the pros use, you should use it too." Of course, it also helps to be as physically fit as the professional football players.

NBA player, Ben Wallace, is another professional athlete who was recently featured in *Muscle & Fitness* for his workout regimen.[32] Ben Wallace, formerly of the Detroit Pistons and traded to the Chicago Bulls in 2006 and now with the Cleveland Cavaliers, plays the power forward position like no other player in the league. The major reason is his strict workout regimen.

In the December 2006 edition of *Muscle & Fitness,* Wallace showcased his workout regimen and described how he became physically fit and powerful as a basketball player. Wallace said: "Lifting weights, you get your body strong and that leads to being strong-minded. I might be hurting, but I know I can do whatever I have to do to bounce back. Time in the weight room can make a good player great. I think that's what separates most of the guys."[33]

It becomes quite apparent from this article on Ben Wallace as well the new Under Armour advertisements that images of physically fit African American athletes help the fitness industry promote, sell, and market their products to a much wider audience, particularly to mainstream American audiences.

What is more fascinating about this emerging trend is that the fitness industry is showing more physically fit physical images of African Americans associated with a number of fitness products, whether it is in sports magazines, sports books, or advertising for fitness apparel, team sports, fitness clubs, and health and fitness programs. The positive impact of these physically fit images in mainstream America helps to dispel the misconceptions that African Americans are not health and fitness conscious; it also helps the African American population view itself as not only participants in the health and fitness industry, but also as leaders and role models for the new type of health and fitness trends emerging in mainstream America and worldwide.

CHAPTER 8

AFRICAN AMERICAN IMAGE IN THE TELEVISION AND MOVIE INDUSTRIES

INTRODUCTION

Recently, I was about to leave a local pharmacy store, when suddenly, the person behind the cash register asked me a simple question: "Do you know who you look like?" Of course, I had an idea, because I have been told that I looked like a former professional football player, Marshall Faulk, and, believe it or not, even Eddie Murphy! Yet the comment that I received from the clerk was not what I expected.

The clerk said that I looked like George Jefferson (actor Sherman Hemsley) from the 1970s and 1980s television show *The Jeffersons*. I could not believe what I'd heard, and I really didn't know how to react. After a momentary pause, I said, "Well, that's a new one on me." I smiled and then left the pharmacy.

On one hand, it was a compliment to be compared with the George Jefferson character because in the show, George Jefferson is a successful African American business man "movin' on up" to a higher income status while also assertively supporting his family. Yet on the other hand, it was embarrassing to be compared with him because he was a smaller, middle-aged African American man who eventually became somewhat caricatural in his over-the-top behavior. It was also embarrassing because this show is over twenty-five years old. However, when I really thought about it, there have not been that many positive African American male role models in successful, long-running television series on the major networks that most Americans have seen, let alone remember. The simple fact is that I really admired George Jefferson's bravado, attitude, and self-assurance as an African American male.

Finally, what I also learned from this look-alike identity experience is that American television is extremely powerful in establishing visual images and our own self-perception of society, but most importantly how our society is perceived by others. These visual images, particularly as they represent specific groups such as African Americans, can either provide a deeper understanding and appreciation of those people, or they can provide more of a misconception and stereotype of a people. Unfortunately, I would have to say that American television and movie industries have historically portrayed African Americans in more of the stereotypical roles, both culturally and physically. It has only been within the past two decades where American television and movies have truly seen and embraced more of the diverse physical images of African Americans.

The next question is, "Why did the television and movie industries take so long to embrace more of the diverse physical images of African Americans?" The answer is really quite simple.

In general in my opinion, the American mainstream television and movie audiences along with the major decision makers who produced these television shows and movies were not culturally ready and willing to see the actual physical images of African Americans on a consistent basis. Therefore, most mainstream American television and movie audiences saw stereotypical physical images of the African American population. In other words, African Americans had to be either overweight, dark-complected, athletic, working-class, or drug–dealing. If African Americans were not in any of these categories, then they were an exception to the rule. Thus, the stereotypical physical images of African Americans were often more preferred and accepted by the American mainstream and, ironically, African American television and movie audiences.

Indeed, even the African American television and movie audiences get trapped into preferring certain physical images of the African American population. That is, if African Americans only see certain physical images of themselves in television shows and at the movies, then they will begin to believe that those few physical images actually represent their population.

That's truly the power of television and the movies—they can actually change and corrupt a people's perception of themselves. This is why it is so important for all of us to examine the cultural impact that television and the movie industry have had on the African American image in the past, the present, and of course the future!

TELEVISION AND THE AFRICAN AMERICAN IMAGE: A CULTURAL HISTORICAL REVIEW

In his book titled *Channeling Blackness: Studies on Television and Race in America*, Darnell Hunt states that popular television is a key medium, one that circulates images and messages around the clock on hundreds of broadcasts, cable, and satellite channels. While network television has steadily lost viewers to cable and other media alternatives over the years, in 2003 the top-rated network programs still attracted between twenty to thirty million viewers each—a figure considerably larger than those for the most popular cable programs.[1]

He further states that, for better or worse, popular television also functions as a central cultural forum in our society. "It serves as social space for the mediated encounters that distinguish the lived experiences of today from those of old, as a place for us to casually sample our fondest desires or our most dreaded fears, as a comfort zone from which we can identify with our heroes (particularly in episodic programs) or affirm our differences from undesirable Others."[2] So one cannot doubt or underestimate the full impact that popular American mainstream television can have on the general population.

A wide variety of positive, physical images of African Americans exists on popular American mainstream television today. African Americans—men, women, girls, and boys—of all body shapes, sizes, and colors are regularly seen on most of the major network television series and particularly on the cable channels. Yet it was not that way at all in the early years of American television.

The first show to have an all-black cast was *The Amos 'n Andy Show*, which originated on radio in the late 1920s. Two European American actors, Freeman Gosden and Charles Correll, mimicked the so-called black dialect, with over-the-top gusto, the humorous exploits of Amos Jones and his gullible associate Andrew "Andy" Brown. The radio show was so successful with American mainstream audience that it endured for decades. In 1951, Gosden and Correll brought *Amos 'n Andy* to television.[3]

Instead of following the minstrel tradition of having European American actors perform in black-face, the show's creators assembled an accomplished, all-black cast—television's first—after an extensive national search. Hunt emphasizes that because most of the actors eventually chosen for the show were veterans of the stage, their delivery was highly stylized, exaggerated, and larger than life. These qualities often combined with clever writing to produce outlandishly funny sequences, particularly those involving the conniving George "Kingfish" Stevens; his shrew of a wife, Sapphire; the crooked lawyer, Calhoun; and the dim-witted janitor, Lightning. The popularity of the television version of *Amos 'n Andy* quickly approached that of the radio.[4]

The physical images and types represented by the main characters on the show were other significant aspects of *The Amos 'n Andy Show*. The main character, Kingfish, was a heavy-set, overweight African American man, while his wife, Sapphire, was a light-skinned, slim African American woman. The other male characters were often medium to dark-complected, slim individuals. What is interesting about the actors' physical types is that they helped to feed into the stereotypical physical images that many mainstream American audiences believed to represent the African American population. Thus this very first all-black cast mainstream American television show of the 1950s on a major network (CBS) established the physical images as well as the cultural images associated with the African American population.

Not surprisingly, these physical and cultural images of African Americans in *The Amos 'n Andy Show* were not accepted by many of the cultural and legal institutions within the African American community. In fact, the National Association for the Advancement of Colored People (NAACP) filed a legal suit against CBS leveling the following charges against the show:

1. It tends to strengthen the conclusion among uninformed and prejudiced people that Negroes are inferior, lazy, dumb, and dishonest.
2. Every character in this one and only show with an all-Negro cast is either a clown or a crook.
3. Negro doctors are shown as quacks and thieves.
4. Negro lawyers are shown as slippery cowards, ignorant of their profession, and without ethics.
5. Negro women are shown as cackling, screaming shrews, in big-mouth close-ups using street slang, just short of vulgarity.
6. All Negroes are shown dodging work of any kind.
7. Millions of white Americans see this *Amos 'n Andy* picture and think the entire race is the same.[5]

The NAACP eventually succeeded in its campaign against *Amos 'n Andy*, and CBS cancelled the show in 1953 at the height of its popularity.

The outcome of this mainstream American television show featuring the first all-black cast highlights the significance that cultural and physical images associated with African Americans play in determining whether African Americans accept them or not. The cultural and physical images that were more in line with the accurate portrayal of African Americans greatly increased its chances for stay and longevity on mainstream American television. Yet the most important impact of *The Amos 'n Andy Show* was that mainstream American television producers and networks had to be more responsible and aware of the African American standards of cultural and physical images associated with African Americans. It was quite obvious that African Americans' standards of appropriate cultural and physical images were different from mainstream Americans' stereotype of cultural and physical images of African Americans. That is the reason why the NAACP and other African American organizations became more involved in the visual and cultural portrayal of African Americans in mainstream American television.

Because of the racial and ethnic climate of the times, subsequent decades witnessed network television make adjustments of their depictions of African Americans. Although mainstream American television in the 1960s included very respectable positive cultural and physical images of African Americans in television shows such as *Julia* (NBC), featuring Diahann Carroll—a slim, light-brown-complected, model-like African American woman—and *I Spy* (NBC), featuring Bill Cosby—a slim, athletic, muscular, medium-brown-complected African American man—the 1970s mainstream American television shows were in direct contrast to those of the 1960s.[6]

In the 1970s, a series of black-oriented situation comedies emerged on mainstream American network television that confronted the gritty realities of inner-city urban life, using humor and comic relief to discuss the relevant issues of the day. Although shows such as *Good Times* (CBS), *Sanford and Son* (NBC), and *The Jeffersons* (CBS) were set firmly in the black world and populated with black characters who reflected the diverse physical types of the African American community (slim, medium- to heavy-set body types for men and women), Hunt emphasizes that they were controlled by white producers to appeal to the largely white television audience.[7] In fact, some critics questioned whether the medium had regressed back to the buffoonish portrayals of the 1950s. Reviewing the 1974 television season, the National Black Feminist Organization had the following comments:

1. Black shows are slanted toward the ridiculous with no redeeming counterimages.
2. Third World peoples are consistently cast in extremes.
3. When blacks are cast as professional people, the characters they portray generally lack professionalism and give the impression that black people are incapable and inferior in such positions.
4. When older persons are featured, black people are usually cast as shiftless derelicts or nonproductive individuals.[8]

Despite the overall popularity of these shows in mainstream America and even within the African American community, it becomes quite apparent that these comments from the National Black Feminist Organization in 1974 reflected a growing concern of the cultural and physical imagery of African Americans on mainstream American television.

Nonetheless, the two television shows that were highly successful on mainstream American television during the 1970s that received praise from the mainstream media as well as all the major African American institutions for their accurate portrayal of African Americans were the miniseries *The Autobiography of Miss Jane Pitman,* starring actress Cicely Tyson, and *Roots,* an adaptation of Alex Haley's book. In particular, *Roots* presented the epic story of the African American odyssey from Africa through slavery to the twentieth century. It brought to millions of mainstream American audiences, for the first time, the story of the horrors of slavery and the noble struggles of African Americans. This television representation of African Americans remained anchored by familiar commitments to economic mobility, family cohesion, private property, and the notion of America as a land of immigrants held together by shared struggles of hardships and ultimate triumph.[9]

The *Roots* miniseries actually contributed significantly to the transformation, in the popular imagination, of the discourse of slavery and American race relations between blacks and whites. Gray states that the popular media discourse about slavery moved from one of almost complete invisibility (never mind structured racial subordination, human degradation, and economic exploitation) to one of ethnicity, immigration, and human triumph. This powerful television epic effectively constructed the story of American slavery from the stage of emotional identifications and attachments to individual characters, family struggles, and the realization of the American dream.[10]

The *Roots* miniseries also contributed significantly to the accurate portrayal of the cultural and physical images associated with Africans and African Americans. The actors and actresses portraying Africans and African Americans reflected the diversity of body types, skin color, and hair texture associated with Africans and African Americans. In fact, the lead actor of the miniseries, LeVar Burton, who played Kunta Kinte, received countless accolades and awards for his convincing physical and acting portrayal of an enslaved African becoming Americanized during the early slavery years in America. Thus if there was one mainstream American television show that got it truly correct in the 1970s culturally and physically, it was the *Roots* miniseries.

In the 1980s, the one black-oriented show that stood out above the rest for eight consecutive years and which is still shown in syndication today is *The Cosby Show,* starring Bill Cosby and Felicia Rashad, a professional African American couple (medical doctor and attorney, respectively) raising four children in the comfortable Brooklyn brownstone neighborhood of New York. In practical terms, the goal of *The Cosby Show* was to provide "positive" and uplifting images of blackness that would correct the distorted images circulated in years past, beginning with stereotypical shows like *Amos 'n Andy* and moving through the ghetto-centric situation comedies of the 1970s.[11] Within a few weeks of its first airing, *The Cosby Show* became an instant hit in mainstream American households as well as in African American homes. Thus, *The Cosby Show* accomplished its major goal, providing positive and uplifting images of blackness that most mainstream Americans and even certain segments of the African American community were not exposed to on a consistent basis.

Hunt notes that the 1990s was marked by a number of important developments and trends: the debut of two new networks (UPN and the WB in 1995) and the increasing segmentation of the television audience; an alarming consolidation of media ownership; the continuing invisibility of other racial and ethnic groups in prime time and a corresponding overrepresentation of African Americans (about sixteen percent of all characters, compared with about twelve percent of the U.S. population);[12] and a significant rise in the number of black-oriented sitcoms. Table 1 shows the dramatic growth of black-themed network shows during the 1990s.

Table 1. Black-Themed Network Television Shows—1990s[13]

Time Line	Black-Themed Network Television Shows
1990–1990	New Attitude (ABC)
	Sugar & Spice (CBS)
1990–1991	Brewster's Place (ABC)
1990–1992	Gabriel's Fire (ABC)
	True Colors (Fox)
1990–1994	In Living Color (Fox)
1991–1992	The Royal Family (CBS)
1991–1993	Rhythm & Blues (NBC)
1991–1994	Roc (Fox)
1992–1993	Here & Now (NBC)
1992–1997	Hangin' with Mr. Cooper (ABC)
1993–1994	Thea (ABC)
1993–1998	Living Single (Fox)
1994–1994	704 Hauser (CBS)
	South Central (Fox)
1994–1995	Me and the Boys (ABC)
1995–1999	In the House (NBC)
	The Wayans Brothers (WB)
	The Parent Hood (WB)
1996–1997	Goode Behavior (UPN)
	Homeboys in Outer Space (UPN)
1996–1998	Sparks (UPN)
1996–2000	Cosby (CBS)
	Malcolm & Eddie (UPN)
1996–2001	The Jamie Foxx Show (WB)
	Moesha (UPN)
1996–2002	The Steve Harvey Show (WB)
1997–1997	Arsenio Hall (ABC)
1997–1998	The Gregory Hines Show (CBS)
1997–1999	Smart Guy (WB)
	Between Brothers (Fox)
1998–1998	The Secret Diary of Desmond Pfeiffer (UPN)
1998–2002	The Hughleys (ABC)
1999–2001	The PJs (WB)
1999–2006	The Parkers (UPN)

Ironically, although most of these black-oriented shows were on the smaller networks, they did reflect the cultural and physical diversity of African American body types and images. For example, the television show *Living Single* featured for the first time, four single, professional, and confident women of various body sizes, hair styles, and skin colors living in an urban setting and dealing with life's issues from young African American women's perspectives. The show centered upon actress Queen Latifah's (Khadijah James) and veteran actress Kim Fields's (Regine Hunter) characters. The show's foundation and concept originated with its producer and creator, Yvette Lee Browser, a young, African American woman herself.[14]

In general, the mainstream American television shows from the 1990s through 2007 displayed more of the cultural and physical diversity of the African American population. Although the major three networks (ABC, CBS, NBC) have stayed away from producing black-oriented television shows since the 1990s, the smaller networks (UPN, WB, and Fox) continue to take the lead in attempting to correctly represent the cultural and physical diversity of African Americans.

MUSIC VIDEOS AND THE AFRICAN AMERICAN WOMEN'S IMAGE

Interestingly, the one major media venue on mainstream American television (MTV, VH1) and black-oriented networks such as Black Entertainment Television (B.E.T) that tended to poorly represent the cultural and physical imagery of African Americans throughout the 1990s and even today are the music videos. The music videos contain imagery that reflects and reproduces the institutional context in which they are produced, and they are permeated by stereotypical controlling images of black womanhood. Several stereotypes emerge in the ways black women's videos are programmed, as well in the content of the videos themselves.[15]

For example, Emerson states that, first, the videos emphasize black women's bodies—primarily bodies that would be considered thin by most standards—but not the variety in body size and weight that is typical of African American women. Second, they construct a one-dimensional black womanhood. Finally, the presence of male sponsors in the videos and a focus on themes of conspicuous consumption and romance further exhibit the types of social constraints faced by young black women.[16] Thus, many music videos still account for the poor physical imagery and stereotypical body types associated with African American women.

Another damaging affect of music videos on the physical imagery and stereotypical body types associated with African American women was excellently illustrated in Stephens and Few's ground-breaking research study titled "The Effects of Images of African American Women in Hip-Hop on Early Adolescents' Attitudes Toward Physical Attractiveness and Interpersonal Relationships." They state that research on images of African American womanhood by women's studies and African American studies scholars has informed our understanding of the ways in which we give meaning to visual cues through theoretical frameworks such as black feminism, womanism, and racial identity development. The integration of these frameworks has created a qualitative body of work that has become a starting point from which to explore African American women's sexuality within the context of African American youth culture.[17] The details that qualitative data impart about African American women's sexuality not only provide descriptions of images, but also give clues into the meaning of sexuality for this population.

Further, the sociohistorical frameworks of race, class, sexual orientation, and gender embedded within sexual images highlight the distinctive identity processes unique to African American women. Remnants of the Jezebel, Mammy, Welfare Mother, and Matriarch images remain, as exemplified by the similar, yet more sexually explicit, images of the Diva, the Gold Digger, the Freak, the Dyke, the Gangster Bitch, the Sister Savior, the Earth Mother, and the Baby Mama.[18] These eight images were found to be widely accepted frameworks used to illustrate beliefs about African American women's sexuality in the heterosexual, male-dominated, African American-based youth culture known as hip-hop.

For example, Stephens and Few describe these eight images as follows:

Diva Image—projects a woman who has sex to enhance her social status, even though she may already be financially independent and middle class or above.

Gold Digger Image—illustrates a woman who intentionally has sex for money or material goods.

Freak Image—portrayed as a woman desiring and engaging in "wild and kinky" sex with a multitude of partners for her own gratification.

Dyke Image—projects a self-sufficient and "hard" woman who has rejected sex with men and may have adopted masculine postures.

Gangster Bitch Image—a "street tough" woman who has sex to demonstrate solidarity with, or to help, her man; she may also be involved in gangs or gang culture.

Sister Savior Image—a pious woman who rejects all but marital, procreative sex for religious reasons.

Earth Mother Image—portrays a woman who has sex for spiritual or nationalistic reasons to show her support for "the race" or the "the nation."

Baby Mama Image—a woman who has had a child by a man but is no longer his partner. She has sex to maintain a financial or emotional connection with the man through the child.

These eight cultural images shape women's sexual identity as well as influence their individual behavior.[19]

To determine whether these eight cultural images influenced adolescent imagery and sexual behavior, Stephens and Few arranged a study to identify African American early adolescents' subjective meanings of African American women's sexuality and how their experiences as members of a marginalized group may influence their understandings. Culturally-based sexual images are projected of African American hip-hop culture.[20]

To explore these culturally-based sexual images, Stephens and Few asked the following research questions about African American adolescent girls' sexuality:

1. In what ways do the eight sexual images reflect attitudes and beliefs about African American women's physical attractiveness and subsequent assumptions about sexuality?
2. How do these beliefs about physical attractiveness inform attitudes toward and beliefs about interpersonal relationships?[21]

In this study, they used qualitative data collection techniques. Qualitative research is rooted in the field of medical anthropology, which examines health beliefs, health care patterns, and health care systems of various cultural and ethnic populations from a biopsychosociocultural perspective. In essence, medical anthropology takes a holistic view of a particular health issue. The use of qualitative methods, particularly interviews or narrative documents, has been instrumental in informing researchers of the various dynamics that shape sexuality, race, and gender interactions.[22] Interviews with youth provide the most direct window into adolescents' sexual experiences through rich descriptions that can detail facts that are not easily quantified.[23]

This study also used purposeful sampling, which involved identifying participants who might give the most comprehensive and knowledgeable information about sexual images in African American youth culture. Fifteen African American early adolescents, aged 11–13, participated in the study (seven boys and eight girls). Data were gathered from both boys and girls as the frameworks for African American adolescents' sexual images are informed through heterosexual relationship expectations.[24]

Additional characteristics of their study were as follows:

1. Participants were recruited from a federally funded after school program designed for low income families.
2. All attended public middle schools.
3. All resided in the southeastern college town all of their lives.
4. None of the participants were currently involved in a romantic or sexual relationship.

5. The majority had never experienced any form of sexual activity.
6. All reported that they had not experienced sexual onset, specifically sexual intercourse.
7. Only four boys and two girls indicated that they had ever kissed or "made out" with a member of the other sex.
8. No participant reported currently being involved in an intimate relationship with a person of the other sex, although several discussed having had "boyfriends" or "girlfriends."
9. The participants described themselves as "brown" or "dark-skinned."
10. None of the participants viewed themselves as "light-skinned."[25]

The procedure for this study used three data collection techniques: (1) semi-structured focus groups, (2) written feedback documentation, and (3) the researchers' notes. These multiple sources of data collection were used in order to triangulate the data and to confirm emergent themes and inconsistencies. The focus groups coincided with the open period of the after-school programming schedule. Participants were brought to a private classroom in the academic area of the facility. Boys and girls were interviewed on separate days.[26]

Some of the major focus group questions included:

1. What kind of messages have you received about African American women's sexuality?
2. What kinds of messages in the media, particularly videos, are being shown about African American women?
3. Are African American women portrayed in the same way as other racial groups when it comes to sexuality?[27]

In addition, each participant was given a handout with an image of a female hip-hop artist who personified the image being discussed. The purpose of the handout was for participants to list beliefs about these images as they related to sexual behaviors and attitudes from the perspective of (1) themselves, (2) their female cohort, and (3) their male cohort. The images were introduced individually, so that participants were not made aware in advance of what images were to be discussed.[28]

Throughout the process, Stephens and Few noted that the researchers made notes about participant-researcher interactions and salient issues that emerged through the focus group discussions. Participant-researcher interactions, body language, subsequent interview questions, and outlines of possible categories, themes, and patterns were also included in the researchers' notes.[29]

From the qualitative data interviews, two significant themes emerged from the sampled adolescents: (1) physical attractiveness and (2) interpersonal relationships. After detailed data analysis, these two themes reflected the beliefs, thoughts, and attitudes of this study's participants.

With regard to physical attractiveness, the eight sexual images provided cues regarding values given to African American female physical attractiveness. Hair texture, skin color, and body image were central to participants' descriptions of appropriate sexual image characteristics. However, mainstream American culture's ideas about physical attractiveness were not expressed. These young women gave less value to westernized standards of beauty than expected.

Here are comments from two participants:

Crystal: "No I think Mary J (dark-skinned artist) is a Diva. You can be darker skin and be beautiful. Like all light-skinned girls are not pretty. People think they are. But not all are. A Diva is about how you carry yourself."

Tracey: "I think (Lauryn Hill) is beautiful. Even with her dreads. Yeah, she is. I like her hair. Yeah, (Lauryn Hill) is beautiful. But I wouldn't put in dreads. I don't want it for me."[30]

Stephens and Few state that it is important to note that the girls often referred to what men found physically attractive in conjunction with what they themselves considered attractive. This was a pattern that did not emerge among the boys' responses. For example, although some of the girls expressed how beautiful they thought representations of the Earth Mother image were, they also acknowledged that men may not perceive that image as attractive for a potential partner. The girls themselves did not like the idea of shaving their hair short or putting in dreadlocks for fear of how unattractive and unfeminine they would be perceived by others, namely boys and men.[31]

All of the girls in the study were also comfortable with their appearance, and none expressed any dissatisfaction. They all expressed happiness with their overall appearance. Some of their comments were:

Leesa: "I'm not super pretty but I'm not ugly. I'm happy, and I think my body is nice."

Crystal: "I'm happy. Even if you don't like something . . . you can get your hair done up nice if you don't like it and feel good."[32]

Stephens and Few also state that the girls' comments regarding men's beliefs about attractive physical traits were accurate. Five of the boys mentioned that they like women with long hair and shapely bodies; the Diva was viewed by seven of the boys as the most beautiful and desirable image. Traditionally, this image is projected as having Westernized features: long, straight hair, slim nose, slender body, and lighter skin. These features were all cited by the boys as attractive.[33]

As for the second theme—interpersonal relationships—it was clear that ideals about potential partners drew on traditional ideals about African American women's sexuality as it relates to the physical attractiveness beliefs, gender expectations, and sexual permissiveness. Stephens and Few note that all eight girls acknowledged that women's appearance is what initially attracts men and is used by men to determine who they choose to pursue. Similarly, six of the seven boys listed physical traits before personality traits to describe ideal sexual partners. They noted that women's physical attributes were key components in their mate selection decision-making processes.

David: "You want to be with a girl that looks good . . . Because then you'll like to see her and be around her with your friends."

Michael: "What you see is what you get, so you pick the prettiest girl."[34]

Stephens and Few state that both male and female participants tended to view men as "sexually-driven" and knowledgeable about sexuality. Participants believed that men would experience sexual activity with a variety of women before marriage. However, all seven of the boys planned to marry a "good" woman. A good woman was perceived as highly feminine and physically attractive. The specific images that boys described as a "good woman" were the Diva and the Sister Savior. Three boys stated they would never have casual sex with a Sister Savior, but would be willing to have a long-term relationship with one in the future.[35]

The sampled boys also stated that the Gangster Bitch was the only one liked in the context of a platonic relationship, not as an image for a sister or mother. The boys wrote that Gangster Bitches were "cool," "funny," "nice," and "just like another boy." Only one girl acknowledged that she saw similarities between herself and this image, although she rejected the usage of the term *Bitch*. Instead, she thought that her desire to hang around and play with boys was because she preferred their forms of play (namely basketball) and because the boys lived in her area. She was not interested in having sexual relationships with them.[36]

As was found among the boys, seven of the eight girls stated that their fathers, brothers, or uncles would want them to be a Diva or a Sister Savior. These girls stated that their male relatives would accept their utilization of these images because they represented what is "good" and "nice" in terms of sexual behaviors and general decorum. All of the girls rejected the possibility of using the Dyke or Freak images around their male relatives because these images projected sexual deviance. Girls were particularly negative in their assessment of the Dyke's sexual behaviors, and referred to them as "nasty" in their written comments.[37]

Despite the positive and high status given to these "good girl" sexual images, girls thought that men could potentially cheat with women who would entice them sexually. The girls unanimously agreed that the boys' favorite images for nonmonogamous intimate relationships would be the Freak and the Diva.

Keisha: "They want the girl who will give them sex and looks good, too. Boys like girls like these and want us to be like them."

Nicole: "I really don't like being friends with Freaks because they give you a bad reputation. If they're your friend and they do something nasty, others might think that you do that. It just gets all out of hand and people get to asking you to do stuff. . . they'll think you are like her when you not. But like her more than you still."[38]

Stephens and Few state that clearly the majority of these eight images do not promote positive women-to-women platonic relationships. Only the Sister Savior was noted by one girl as "easy to make friends with." It is interesting that boys were aware of the tensions these images could create among girls. Boys thought that their female cohort used these sexual images to accept or reject peers. They indicated that girls would be jealous of other girls who enacted highly sexualized or physically attractive images (e.g., Diva, Freak).

Wayne: "I think they really want to be like Diva and hate the girls that do dress like that."

Anthony: "Girls get jealous of other girls just because we're not paying attention to them."[39]

In conclusion, Stephens and Few state that the results of their study with regard to perceptions of physical attractiveness and interpersonal relationships provide evidence that identity development does not occur in a vacuum. In this study, a space was observed where social constructions of race and gender intersected to create, maintain, and reproduce sexual identities. These adolescents used self-comparison and relied on messages about appropriate or desirable sexual and physical traits from peers, media, and parents to develop perceptions of their sexuality and beliefs about their own sexual needs.[40]

In particular, body size and shape emerged as important aspects of physical attractiveness. Stephens and Few found that boys spent a considerable amount of time discussing the shapes and sizes of African American women's bodies. It was clear that traditional European American body shapes were not considered the most attractive.[41] Rather, these boys preferred the more curvaceous body types typically associated with African American women.[42] Buttocks that were "large and round," "big breasts," and "thick thighs" were listed as ideal in the comments written by the boys. Within the African American community and other communities of color, this attitude is common among men. This male focus on parts of women's bodies, rather than the whole, disregards a woman's identity as a person. This process makes it easier for men to sexualize and objectify women without consideration of their feelings or desires.[43]

Interestingly, the discussion of body type ideals was not as extensive or as detailed among the girls. Stephens and Few contend that this may be because, unlike European American women, African American women often report that "looking good" is related more to public image and personality than to weight, a belief that was articulated by two participants in the present study.[44] This may explain why African American women are more positive and flexible in their ideal body than European American women are.[45]

African American body types, skin color, and hair texture clearly served as identifying racial markers of beauty. Overall, Stephens and Few found that boys gave more value to Westernized standards of beauty than the girls did by selecting those sexual images that embodied such traits as long hair and lighter skin as more attractive. The girls indicated that all skin shades and textures of hair can be attractive; the personality of the individual is what is most important.[46]

Finally, Stephens and Few state that it is clear that traditional Western standards of beauty continue to be normalized and valued among these participants despite changing role models of attractiveness in mainstream American society. Those sexual images that embody these traits (e.g., long hair, shapely yet slender build, lighter skin) were generally viewed as the most attractive.[47] The ways in which hip-hop culture specifically promotes these ideals must be explored further in future research. This is particularly important given the centrality of and value given to women's physical appearance in music videos and other expressions in hip-hop culture.

MOVIES AND THE AFRICAN AMERICAN IMAGE:
A CULTURAL-HISTORICAL REVIEW

Hollywood movies have always exhibited a sort of cultural politics in their treatment of ethnicity, but their usage of African Americans has always seemed more resistant to change, even under the pressure of social crises. The reason for this inertia derives from the circumstances of their production. In Dates and Barlow's *Split Image: African Americans in the Mass Media*, they state that by the teens of the twentieth century, movie making had been rationalized. First movie making consisted of a cartel of patent holders. Then, movie making involved filmmakers, producers, and eventually studios. Interestingly, all serving a distributive system that played to audiences whose expectations had been shaped by normalizing forces such as advertising, journalistic reviewing, lush picture palaces, a system of promoting stars, and particularly a studio system that routinized production into a classical cinema of surefire, risk-free, cost-effective products that fulfilled mainstream American audiences' anticipations of style, texture, and satisfying happy endings.[48]

The challenge for African Americans would be to battle against such apparently ironclad determination through protest, intervention in Hollywood, and indigenous filmmaking. One of the very first movies that motivated African

Americans to challenge mainstream American movie makers was D. W. Griffith's 1915 film, *The Birth of a Nation*. The basic premise of the movie was that it celebrated the institution of slavery and portrayed African Americans as vicious, lustful, corrupt people.[49]

The furor surrounding the film prompted protest and criticism but also galvanized a fledging black independent film sector into action. Early black independent films, such as *Birth of a Race* (1918), *The Realization of a Negro's Ambition* (1916), *Trooper of Troop K* (1916), and *The Homesteader* (1919), attempted to correct the balance of overly negative and stereotypical portraits from mainstream American movies by supporting and articulating black pride and ambitions.[50] Karen Ross, author of *Black and White Media: Black Images in Popular Film and Television*, states that although these early efforts were low budget and often technically unsophisticated, their importance lay in demonstrating the feasibility of a black cinema that was attractive to a black audience, a cinema that showed them realistic and authentic portraits of the race. The insulting stereotypes that were popular in the early years of film were all that black filmgoers of the time could otherwise expect to see of themselves. Thus the sight of educated black professionals living a relatively successful American life, albeit with the odd problem of racism here and there, was clearly welcomed by a black audience eager for more positive reflections of itself.[51]

One of the earliest black film makers was Oscar Micheaux, who produced movies for approximately thirty years. He is considered the originator of the black action films. Micheaux founded the Micheaux Film and Book Company in 1918. His films were situated in urban settings and often dealt with the kind of race-specific issues that his black contemporaries ignored. He is attributed with making more than thirty films from around 1919 to 1948, many of which were based on his books. Micheaux films (*The Homesteader*, *Within Our Gates* (1920), *The Gunsaulus Mystery* (1921), *The Brute* (1920), and *Body and Soul* (1924)) portrayed the lived experiences of black communities, such as lynching, interracial relationships, gambling, and prostitution. His dramatic considerations of such intimate and controversial subjects were attractive to a newly urbanized and aware black audience.[52]

In particular, *Body and Soul* featured the film debut of one of the greatest African American stage and film actors, Paul Robeson. In this film, Robeson played two roles: a good guy who is the backbone of a local black bourgeois community, and a shifty preacher intent on taking advantage of his black flock in general and the demure young heroine in particular.[53] The film caused a degree of controversy in the black community because it examined the role of black preachers and to what degree they instigate divisiveness in the community.

As for actor Paul Robeson, he was multitalented. Not only was he an actor, Robeson was an academic scholar, athlete, singer, writer, linguist, and civil rights activist. His physical appearance was striking and imposing because he was tall and physically fit. Therefore, Robeson's physical imagery (tall, intelligent, confident, assertive) was in direct contrast to the physical imagery that most mainstream American movie producers and audiences perceived as associated with an African American male (average height, slow-witted, nonassertive, lazy).

Yet during the Depression years, many actors and black independent filmmakers such as Micheaux suffered in their ability to maintain autonomy. In fact, Micheaux had to reform his company in 1929 into a partnership with white financing. Although Micheaux still produced movies such as *Daughter of the Congo* (1930) and *God's Step Children* (1937), he continued to receive criticism from critics who said that his films no longer reflected the "blackness" of African American life.[54]

Throughout the 1940s and 1950s, numerous black performers starred in black films, and because the dimensions of racism were largely removed from film narratives, the resulting portraits of black community life were celebrations of a particular black style rather than accurate descriptions of life for most African Americans. Between 1910 and 1950, more than 150 independent film companies were organized for the specific purposes of producing black-cast films for black audiences, and of this number, slightly more than one-third were owned and operated by black individuals and partnerships.[55]

During this time period, two pioneering African American women not only made their impact in black films but also crossed over to mainstream American Hollywood films. They were Hattie McDaniel and Lena Horne. Although these two actresses were completely different in physical appearance and the types of roles each played, they nonetheless opened up new doors for so many more African American women than ever before because of their sacrifice and efforts to make a difference in mainstream American Hollywood.

For example, Hattie McDaniel was a heavy-set, dark-complected African American woman who often played the maids or the mammy in major motion pictures. After several years in these stereotypical roles, Hattie McDaniel finally got the role which made her a household name. In 1939, she was cast in *Gone with the Wind,* starring Vivien Leigh, Clark Gable, and African American star Butterfly McQueen. McDaniel's role as the sassy servant who repeatedly scolds her mistress, Scarlett O'Hara (Vivien Leigh) and scoffs at Rhett Butler (Clark Gable) won her the 1939 Academy Award for Best Supporting Actress, making her the first African American to win an Oscar. Several years later she starred in an ABC television hit comedy show, *Beulah*. Although she received much criticism from African American organizations for taking these stereotypical roles as maids and servants in major motion pictures and even television shows, she still goes down in history as being the first African American to receive an Oscar as well as the first black Oscar winner honored with a United States Postal Service stamp in 2006.[56]

Another African American woman who crossed over to mainstream American Hollywood was Lena Horne. Horne became the first African American performer to sign a long-term contract with a major Hollywood studio, MGM, and later became famous for her rendition of *Stormy Weather* in the movie of the same name. Barbara Summers, author of *Skin Deep: Inside the World of Black Fashion Models*, says that perhaps no single woman has been a more enduring representative of black beauty than Lena Horne. Her career as a singer and actress for over sixty years has given her a unique platform from which to view the world—and to be viewed. The flawless copper complexion, the long, silky hair, the glistening smile, the sophisticated manner, all animated a beauty that seemed somewhere to be making fun of itself. While cabaret and movie audiences gasped at her irresistible appeal, the black world shouted "Yes! At last, one of us." She was the first glamorous black Hollywood star.[57]

Later in the 1950s and 1960s, new African American stars continued to cross over to mainstream American Hollywood. Sidney Poitier took on challenging astereotypical roles for an African American male. In movies such as the *Deviant Ones (1958); A Raisin in the Sun (1961); To Sir, With Love (1966); Lilies of the Field (1963)*; and *Guess Who's Coming to Dinner (1967)*, Poitier captivated mainstream American Hollywood audiences with his classy style, confidence, timing, witty communication, and good looks. No longer did African American males have to play the stereotypical roles of the past and only be supporting actors. With Sidney Poitier, African American males could definitely be the strong lead while also showing a wide range of acting styles.

Black filmmakers renewed their interest in making films that reflected the social conditions and civil rights issues of the 1960s and 1970s. Independent filmmakers such as Melvin Van Peebles (*Sweet Sweetback's Baadasssss Song*, 1971), Gordon Parks (*Shaft*, 1971), Gordon Parks, Jr. (*Super Fly*, 1972), and Jack Starrett (*Cleopatra Jones*, 1973) reminded African Americans and particularly mainstream American Hollywood producers that there were still other ways to interpret the African American lifestyle.

Continuing that same tradition of African American filmmaking are today's ground-breaking black filmmakers such as Spike Lee, John Singleton, Bill Duke, Wilson Bell, Robert Townsend, Tim Reid, Tyler Perry, and Oprah Winfrey. Spike Lee's *Malcolm X* (1992), *She's Gotta Have It* (1986), *School Daze* (1988), *Do the Right Thing* (1989), *Inside Man* (2006); John Singleton's *Boyz n the Hood* (1992), *Poetic Justice* (1993), *Higher Learning* (1995), *Four Brothers* (2005); Bill Duke's *A Rage in Harlem* (1991), *Hoodlum* (1997), *The Boy Who Painted Christ Black* (1996); Wilson Bell's *Joe Willlie's Friend* (2005); Robert Townsend's *Hollywood Shuffle* (1987) and *The Five Heartbeats* (1991); Tim Reid's *Once Upon a Time When We Were*

Colored (1996), *Asunder* (1998), *For Real* (2003); Tyler Perry's *Diary of a Mad Black Woman* (2005), *Madea's Family Reunion* (2006), *Why Did I Get Married* (2008), *Tyler Perry's Meet the Browns* (2008); and producer Oprah Winfrey's *Beloved* (1998), *The Great Debaters* (2007) follow the tradition of the very first black filmmakers by examining the cultural issues in the African American community that are often overlooked.

Of particular note is Spike Lee's *School Daze*. It is set in a black southern college and examines color consciousness among college students and the friction between two groups of students—the Wanna-bes and the Jigaboos. The men are allowed to be explicitly political whereas the women are destined to remain locked in a destructive conflict, arguing spitefully about the merits of darker or lighter skin, straight or nappy hair, and who has authority to claim an authentic African ancestry. Ross states that the focus on the politics of hair is particularly interesting in the contemporary context where hair style has once again become the site for expressing black identity and pride.[58]

CONCLUSION

Currently, the dichotomy between mainstream American and black Hollywood film industries still exists. The fact that this dual movie-making system, in which both movie industries create, develop, market, and promote films for their respective audiences, continues to exist in America is another example of the duality in which our American society operates.

Yet an interesting trend has been developing among mainstream American and black moviegoers. Although there is no specific data on this trend, apparently, more mainstream American moviegoers are going to the newly released predominantly African American cast movies than ever before. It may be hard for the average film critic or moviegoer to believe, but box office numbers do not lie.

For example, in 2007, Academy Award-nominated actor Eddie Murphy earned the top spot in the North American box office rankings with a $33.7 million haul for the movie *Norbit*. The Dreamworks film marks Murphy's highest-grossing live-action opener and the fourteenth number one hit of his career (www.blacktalentnews.com/artman/publish/cat_index_33.shtml). The comedy, which was written by Eddie and his older brother, Charlie Murphy, averaged $10,759 from 3,136 theaters. Dreamworks also scored big with Eddie Murphy in *Dreamgirls*, which topped the $100 million dollar mark, and which earned new African American actress and singer Jennifer Hudson a Best Supporting Actress Award in 2007 (www.blacktalentnews. com/artman/ publish/article_1131.shtml).

Not surprisingly, Academy Award winning actor Denzel Washington, who starred in *American Gangster,* along with Russell Crowe, won its opening weekend box office premier at $46.3 million (www.blacktalentnews.

com/artman/publish/article_1572.shtml). Based upon a real-life drug king-pin in Harlem in the early 1970s, *American Gangster* opened in 3,054 the-aters and generated an amazing average of $15,175 per location. The moviegoer turnout was diverse, with about 44 percent of the audience white, 36 percent black, and 10 percent Hispanic according to studio exit surveys. Moreover, 53 percent of the audience was female due primarily to the lure of Denzel Washington and Russell Crowe[59] (www.blacktalentnews.com/artman/publish/article_1572.shtml).

Additionally, the dance flick *Stomp the Yard* debuted in the number one spot, earning $25.4 million over the four-day Martin Luther King Jr. holi-day weekend in 2007, and averaging $12,872 from only 2,051 theaters. The Sony Screen Gems dance flick, despite no major stars and a $14 mil-lion budget, stomped out the three-week reign of *Night at the Museum*. Strong turnout by black moviegoers—who accounted for nearly two-thirds of the audience according to Sony—pushed *Stomp the Yard* over the top (www.blacktalentnews.com/artman/publish/cat_index_33.shtml). Accord-ing to studio research, blacks accounted for nearly two-thirds of the audi-ence, females made up 59 percent of the crowd, while 62 percent were over eighteen years of age. In addition to that particular weekend's movie open-ings (January 12–15, 2007), three of the top five films that weekend fea-tured predominantly African American casts, and a fourth was driven by African American megastar Will Smith (www.blacktalentnews.com/artman/publish/cat_index_33.shtml).[60]

Finally, an article in the *Chicago Tribune* titled "African American Films Ride 'Cosby Effect,'" talks about how mainstream American Hollywood is taking note of movies centered on African American middle class. Specifi-cally, columnist Terry Armour contends that the latest set of movies depict-ing middle-to-upper middle class African American life (Tyler Perry's *Why Did I Get Married?* and Preston Whitmore's *This Christmas*) are proving there is an audience for these types of movies[61] (www.blacktalentnews.com/artman/publish/cat_index_33.shtml).

Willie Packer said the following about the current wave of African American family-themed movies:

A studio's traditional thinking was if you want to pull in an urban audience, you need to have a hip-hop element. Over the past 10 or 15 years, hip-hop was a new and emerging form that pulled in that core African American audience as well as had that crossover potential. It was a business decision more than anything. What is happening now—and it's a great time as far as I'm concerned to be making films about the African American experience—is Hollywood realizes that there is an audience out there that doesn't regularly see themselves on film.[62]

Regina King, who starred in NBC's *227* during the 1980s and was the lead actress in the movie *This Christmas,* is cited by Armour for her comments on Hollywood's current wave of interest in African American family scripts. She specifically said:

At the end of the day, it just comes down—to the studios—to dollars and cents. If they see these movies make money within weeks of each other, I guarantee there will be a person at every studio saying, "Where's that script that somebody mailed here a year ago?" That's the way it is because, unfortunately, everybody wants to be first at being second in Hollywood. They don't want to be the first one to try it. They want to be the first one to have that second success story.[63]

Thus it becomes quite apparent in the mainstream American movie and television industries today that the African American image in all of its physical and cultural diversity is finally being recognized, accepted, and embraced at a whole new societal and cultural level. If this cultural revolution in the film and television industries continues, then someday we will all truly be considered American, and African Americans will not have to live in this duality within our own country that we lived and died for from the very first days of our arrival.

On a personal note, if this cultural revolution continues in the film and television industries, then maybe I will no longer be told that I only look like George Jefferson from the *Jeffersons*! There is always hope!

CHAPTER 9

AFRICAN AMERICAN IMAGE
AND POLITICS

INTRODUCTION

If you ask many of the political experts today, they would contend that there is a cultural revolution occurring within the world of politics, particularly as it relates to African Americans. Regardless of the individual politician's political affiliation, the image of the African American politician has dramatically changed from one that was based on civil rights issues to one that is based on mainstream American issues.

In 2001, even *Jet Magazine* (an African American–focused magazine) noticed this cultural revolution happening to African Americans in politics. *Jet Magazine* stated that colossal changes had catapulted African Americans from the "back of the bus" into the driver's seat at every level of government. In just the past fifty years, African Americans have gone from having no African American governors or major-city mayors to the first elected governor in L. Douglas Wilder (Virginia, 1989) and first big-city mayors in Carl Stokes (Cleveland, 1967) and Richard Hatcher (Gary, Indiana, 1967).

African Americans have witnessed Thurgood Marshal (1967) and Clarence Thomas (1991) take their places as Supreme Court Judges in the nation's highest court. Additionally, African Americans have watched their political influence in Congress swell from two African Americans in 1951 to a power block nearly forty members strong in 2001. Moreover, the exceptional achievements of the first African American women to hold major political offices, such as Representative Shirley Chisholm (1968; presidential candidate, 1972), Senator Carol Moseley Braun (1992), and Sharon Pratt Kelly (mayor of Washington, DC, 1990) have opened the door for other African American women to excel in politics as well.[1]

More recently, two political figures have truly challenged African Americans' and mainstream Americans' image of the typical African American politician. They are Senator Barack Obama, who is also a 2008 Democratic presidential candidate, and former National Security Advisor (2001–2005) and current Secretary of State since 2005, Condoleezza Rice. Although these two politicians represent opposing parties, and one was elected (Obama) whereas the other was appointed (Rice), both are quite similar with respect to the images they project and how these images are perceived by African Americans and mainstream Americans. We will discuss this very significant image issue as it relates to African American politicians later in this chapter.

Therefore, it is not surprising that in today's political arena, Americans are searching for a new type of politician who may look different from them yet shares their core values and issues. That's why many political experts foresee even more African Americans becoming not only a part of the local and national political system, but also representing larger segments of the African American and mainstream American populations.

THE TRADITIONAL IMAGE OF BLACK POLITICS

Political anthropology is the branch of anthropology that studies political organization—the roles and processes that societies have for making decisions, mobilizing action, settling disputes, enforcing social norms, and choosing leaders.[2] Although I am not a political anthropologist, I have always been intrigued by politics in general and particularly how African Americans have had to develop their own type of political organizations and political leaders within American society.

The study of black politics is the study of the purposeful activity of African American people to acquire, use, and maintain power.[3] The dimensions of black politics are internal and external. They characterize a struggle for power, that is, the realization and defense of African American people's objective interests and volition. This struggle for power reflects historical tensions and constraints between African Americans and European Americans, as well as within each group. These tensions and constraints concerning optimum strategies for control and liberation are grounded in the dominant-dominated relationship of the two groups.[4]

According to Hill, black politics has always been burdened with this problem of duality, a duality in the sense that African Americans are constantly negotiating whether to become more a part of mainstream American politics or to be solely centered upon African American political structures, institutions, leaders, and issues. Historically, this problem of duality has been manifested as a conflict between inclusion and communal obligations; between integration, desegregation, and separatism; and between the yearning for universality and for black particularity. African

American leaders who struggled with this dual agenda in our American political system were Harriet Tubman, Frederick Douglass, Marcus Garvey, Booker T. Washington, W. E. B. Du Bois, Medgar Evers, Shirley Chisholm, Angela Davis, Malcolm X, and Dr. Martin Luther King, Jr.[5]

Some political experts would say that this issue of duality continues to exist in black politics, and its effects are as follows:

- It has hampered political development in the African American community.
- It has forced bad political decisions in the African American community.
- It has forced black politics into a dependent, reactive posture.[6]

Are there any merits to this claim of duality associated with African American politics today and in the past, and if so, how does it influence our image of those African Americans who addressed this issue of duality within their own political positions and/or campaigns? To answer these two very important questions, let's review some of the major sociocultural, historical, and political events that have occurred since 1951 as they relate to African Americans in American mainstream politics.

SOCIOCULTURAL, HISTORICAL, POLITICAL EVENTS AND AFRICAN AMERICANS

What follows are highlights of significant national and regional political events from 1951–2001 that dramatically influenced the African American and mainstream American political landscapes. These political events also influenced the overall image associated with African Americans.

1951–1959

- December 31, 1953—Hulan Jack becomes the first African American to hold a major city elective post when he is sworn in as Manhattan Borough president.
- November 2, 1954—Charles C. Diggs Jr. of Detroit is elected Michigan's first African American congressman.
- July 9, 1955—E. Frederic Morrow is named administrative aide to President Dwight Eisenhower, becoming the first African American named to an executive post in the White House.
- February 5, 1958—Clifton R. Wharton Sr., diplomat, is confirmed as minister to Romania, becoming the first African American to head a U.S. embassy in Europe.

1960–1969

- November 10, 1960—Andrew Hatcher is named President Kennedy's associate press secretary.

- January 3, 1961—Representative Adam Clayton Powell, Jr., of New York is named the first African American chair of the House Education and Labor Committee.
- November 3, 1964—John Conyers, Jr., of Detroit is elected to Congress.
- February 23, 1965—Constance Baker Motley is elected Manhattan Borough president and the first African American woman to hold a top post in a major city.
- March 9, 1966—Andrew F. Brimmer becomes first African American to serve on the Board of Governors of the Federal Reserve.
- November 8, 1966—Edward W. Brooke is elected to the U.S. Senate, becoming the first African American elected to the Senate by popular vote.
- August 30, 1967—Thurgood Marshall is confirmed as first African American Supreme Court Justice.
- November 7, 1967—Carl B. Stokes of Cleveland and Richard G. Hatcher of Gary, Indiana, become the first African Americans elected mayors of major U.S. cities in the twentieth century.
- August 28, 1968—the Reverend Channing E. Phillips becomes the first African American nominated for president at a major national political convention.
- November 5, 1968—Shirley Chisholm of New York is the first African American woman representative elected to Congress, and a record number of African Americans (10) are elected to the 91st Congress that year. Joining Chisholm were two first-time representatives, William L. Clay (MO) and Louis Stokes (OH), and six incumbents: John Conyers (MI), William L. Dawson (IL), Charles C. Diggs (MI), Augustus Hawkins (CA), Robert N. C. Nix (PA), and Adam Clayton Powell, Jr. (NY).

1970–1979

- November 3, 1970—Twelve African Americans are elected to the 92nd Congress, including five new congressmen: George W. Collins (IL), Ronald Dellums (CA), Ralph H. Metcalfe (IL), Parren Mitchell (MI), and Charles Rangel (NY).
- February 2, 1971—Congressional Black Caucus (CBC) is formed by African Americans in the U.S. House.
- January 25, 1972—Representative Shirley Chisholm makes a bid for the U.S. presidency.
- June 24, 1972—Yvonne Braithwaite Burke, California assemblywoman, is named cochair of Democratic National Convention of 1972, the first African American to chair a national political convention.
- November 1972—Sixteen African Americans are elected to Congress, including three newcomers: Barbara Jordan (TX), Yvonne Braithwaite Burke (CA), and Andrew Young (GA). Young later would become a U.S. ambassador and mayor of Atlanta.

- December 1972—Attorney Jewel Lafontant becomes the first African American woman named deputy solicitor general of the United States.
- May 29, 1973—Thomas Bradley is elected first African American mayor of Los Angeles.
- October 16, 1973—Maynard Jackson becomes first African American mayor of Atlanta.
- November 6, 1973—Coleman Young is elected first African American mayor of Detroit.
- November 1974—State Senator Mervyn M. Dymally of California and State Senator George L. Brown of Colorado become the first African American lieutenant governors in the twentieth century. Harold Ford of Memphis, Tennessee, is elected to the U.S. House. Henry E. Parker is elected treasurer for Connecticut.
- July 12, 1976—Representative Barbara Jordan of Texas gives main address at the Democratic National Convention, becoming first African American keynote speaker of a national political convention.
- December 21, 1976—Patricia Roberts Harris is named U.S. Secretary of Housing and Urban Development by President Carter, becoming the first African American woman to hold a cabinet post. In 1979, she is named Health, Education, and Welfare secretary and becomes the first African American to hold two successive Cabinet posts.

1980–1989

- October 1981—Andrew Young becomes the second African American mayor of Atlanta. Edward M. McIntyre is elected first African American mayor of Augusta, Georgia.
- November 1981—Thurman L. Milner is elected mayor of Hartford, Connecticut, and James Chase is elected mayor of Spokane, Washington. Four new African American congressmen are elected: Mervyn Dymally (CA), Augustus Savage (IL), Harold Washington (IL), and George W. Crockett, Jr. (MI).
- April 29, 1983—Representative Harold Washington is sworn in as first African American mayor of Chicago.
- November 3, 1983—Rev. Jesse L. Jackson, Sr., announces bid for U.S. presidency, and his campaign generates unprecedented attention.
- November 8, 1983—W. Wilson Goode becomes first African American mayor of Philadelphia.
- March 13, 1984—Republican James L. Usry is elected first African American mayor of Atlantic City, NJ.
- October 15, 1986—Edward Perkins confirmed as America's first African American ambassador to South Africa.

- November 1986—Four new African American Congressmen are elected: Mike Espy, Mississippi's first African American since Reconstruction, Rev. Floyd Flake (NY), John Lewis (GA), and Kweisi Mfume (MD).
- November 3, 1987—Kurt L. Schmoke is elected mayor of Baltimore.
- November 7, 1989—L. Douglas Wilder is elected governor of Virginia, becoming first African American governor of any of the United States.

1990–2001

- September 11, 1990—Sharon Pratt Kelly is elected mayor of Washington, D.C., the first African American woman to head a major U.S. city.
- June 18, 1991—Wellington Webb is elected mayor of Denver.
- July 1, 1991—Clarence Thomas is nominated to the Supreme Court. In October, he is confirmed as the 106th Supreme Court Justice and only the 2nd African American to serve in post.
- November 3, 1991—The Congressional Black Caucus (CBC) gained 16 new members in the 103rd Congress, expanding to 40 members, then the largest bloc of African Americans in Congress in history.
- November 3, 1992—Carol Moseley Braun of Chicago becomes the first African American female senator.
- December 12–21, 1992—Newly elected President Bill Clinton appoints African Americans to his cabinet and a record number of minorities to key positions, including Secretary of Commerce Ron Brown, Hazel O'Leary (Energy), Mike Espy (Agriculture), and Joycelyn Elders (Surgeon General), who later was succeeded by David Satcher. Other appointees named during the Clinton administration were Rodney Slater (Transportation), Jesse Brown (Veterans Affairs), who later was succeeded by Togo West, and Alexis Herman (Labor).
- November 2, 1993—Sharon Sayles Belton is elected first African American mayor of Minneapolis.
- December 12, 1995—Jesse Jackson, Jr., of Chicago is elected to Congress.
- June 3, 1997—Harvey Johnson is elected first African American mayor of Jackson, Mississippi.
- January 20, 2001—Colin Powell, former head of the Joint Chiefs of Staff, is confirmed by Senate as U.S. Secretary of State.
- January 20, 2001—Stanford University political science professor Condoleezza Rice becomes the first woman in history to serve as national security advisor for a U.S. President. She would serve as Secretary of the State beginning in 2005.[7]

The primary purpose in reviewing and highlighting these sociocultural, historical, and political events as they relate to African Americans in newly elected or appointed positions throughout the United States is to not only show the groundbreaking emergence and significant increase of African Americans in top-level political positions, but also to recognize how these particular elected and appointed positions during each time period influenced the overall image that African Americans as well as mainstream Americans associated with African Americans in politics.

The duality issue associated with black politics was and still is an issue for many African Americans. Many of the elected African Americans of the past were elected primarily because of the surge of African American voters in particular districts throughout the country. Once the voting base associated with African American politicians became more mobilized and asserted its power, more African Americans politicians were elected and appointed in local and national districts.

Yet during this time period, many African American politicians gradually expanded beyond their African American voting base and captured a larger percentage of the mainstream American voters. In fact, it was this mainstream American voting base that allowed many more African American politicians to achieve higher-ranking public offices such as mayors, U.S. representatives, and U.S. senators. Thus African Americans not only widened their voting base, but they also opened up more opportunities for elected and appointed positions.

The images that are associated with most people from the past fifty years regarding African Americans are:

1. African American men are very much involved in mainstream American politics.
2. African American women are also very much involved in mainstream American politics.
3. African Americans have increased their political clout substantially during the past fifty years.
4. African Americans are very much involved in both political parties—Democratic and Republican.
5. African Americans were greatly influenced by the civil rights movements of 1950s and 1960s to become more involved in mainstream American politics.

AFRICAN AMERICAN WOMEN

Of all the various images associated with African Americans in politics during this time period, one particular trend was noteworthy—the dramatic increase of African American women in politics. The first African American woman to be elected to a seat in a state legislature was Crystal Bird Fauset, chosen in 1938 to represent Philadelphia in the Pennsylvania legislature.[8] However, it was not until 1952 that an African American woman, Cora Brown of Michigan, became a state senator. In 1969, only 131 African American women held elective office, making up only 10 percent of the total number of black elected officials. During the period 1976–1986, the number of African American women elected to office more than doubled, from 684 to 1,469, making up 27 percent of the 5,384 African American elected officials. Not surprisingly, a majority of the African American women (54%) were concentrated in the South. States with the largest number of African American elected officials are Michigan with ninety-two, followed by New York with eighty-seven, Illinois with seventy-five, and California and Mississippi, each with seventy-one. The District of Columbia, with 113 African American elected officials, had more African American women (including advisory neighborhood commissioners) than any of the states.[9]

Harmon-Martin states that the kinds of elective offices held by African American women have changed since 1977. In 1977, they held 263 education-related offices, that is, positions on state education agencies: college, university, and local school boards; and as superintendents of schools. By 1986, this focus had shifted, and the greatest concentration of African American women in elected positions was at the municipal level. Municipal governing bodies accounted for 45 percent or 697 positions, excluding female mayors. The greater presence of African American women at the municipal level has enhanced their opportunity to capture the office of mayor. Whereas in 1975 there were only nine African American women mayors, in 1986 there were forty, and twenty-nine of them were located in the South. In 1986, African American women, like African American officials generally, were clustered in municipal- and education-related positions. There were also seventy-eight women who were state senators and representatives.[10]

Although African American women have increased their presence in a number of elected offices across the country, they are least visible at the national level. Only one African American woman became senator— Carol Moseley Braun—and the number of African American women at the House of Representatives continues to remain relatively low. Despite the pioneering efforts of Shirley Chisholm (1968), Barbara Jordan (1972), and Yvonne Braithwaite Burke (1972), African American women still experience unique obstacles in entering and succeeding in the political arena.[11]

For example, the Center for the American Woman and Politics conducted an exploratory study titled "Black Women's Routes to Elective Office" to identify factors that facilitate or obstruct African American women's entry into the political arena. The findings of the study reflect the ways in which African American female elected officials have met the challenge of the double jeopardy of race and sex discrimination in order to succeed in a political arena long dominated by mainstream European American men. The study reveals the following:

1. African American women elected officials are more likely than either women overall or men to have attended college, and in many cases they hold advanced degrees.
2. African American women are only slightly less likely than men to be lawyers and more likely than women overall to be lawyers and public administrators.
3. Women overall acquire greater political experience than do men before running successfully for office, and African American women acquire even more experience.
4. African American women are more likely than women overall to have worked in political campaigns before running for office. They also evaluate their campaign experience as critically important in their decisions to run for office.
5. African American women more often than women overall rely on the support of individuals and organizations, specifically women and women's organizations, in order to arrive at their current positions as elected officials. In fact, African American women more often name women as their role models and mentors encouraging them in their political activism.
6. African American women elected officials are less likely than women overall to be married, more likely to have supportive spouses if married, and much less likely to have children.
7. African American women, like women overall, identify a concern with issues, especially social and political issues, as a motivating factor in their decision to run for office.[12]

Overall, this study concludes that African American women's routes to office are influenced by distinctive factors. These race-specific distinctive factors were listed as follows:

- African American women's groups, civil rights group, and church-related groups play an important role in African American women's political activism.
- The desire to represent minorities or to address civil rights issues is one main reason they ran for office.
- The ability to combat discrimination is an important factor in their decision to run for office.[13]

The results of this center's study has begun to answer some questions about the ways in which the experiences of African American female elected officials are different from the experiences of other female elected officials.

African American women's experiences are shaped not only by gender, but also by race, and more research is needed to help separate the effects of race and sex as well as to identify the aspects of African American women's experiences that are the results of the interaction of both.[14]

CURRENT IMAGE OF AFRICAN AMERICANS IN POLITICS

As stated earlier in this chapter, the current image of African Americans in mainstream American politics has significantly changed over the past few years. Gone are the days in which African American politicians touted their civil rights credentials and agendas as though they were special badges of honor and status that only African Americans achieved. The old brigade includes Congressmen Charles Rangel (NY), John Lewis (GA), Bobby Rush (IL), Congresswoman Maxine Waters (CA), Reverend Al Sharpton, and one-time Democratic presidential candidate Reverend Jesse Jackson; these men and women, who regularly protested for civil rights issues, were considered street smart.

Currently African American politicians strive to assert more of their commonality with the mainstream populous and less with their African American base. A recent article titled "The New Black Brigade: Today's African American Politicians Have an Energy All Their Own" suggested that young African American politicians such as former U.S. Senate candidate Harold Ford, Jr., and U.S. Senator and presidential candidate Barack Obama are part of a new guard of black leadership that is just waiting to burst forth. Polished, suave, handsome, and highly educated, Ford and particularly Barack Obama target a wide range of ethnic groups and have downplayed racial identification and racial appeal. In fact, Obama has been more successful than the older African American politicians in garnering crossover votes, while also recognizing a need to maintain the votes of his African American constituency.[15]

For example, Barack Obama, the son of a Kenyan father and a white American mother and best selling author of two books—*Dreams from My Father: A Story of Race and Inheritance* and *The Audacity of Hope: Thoughts on Reclaiming the American Dream*—differs markedly from the typical African American politician. When Obama delivered his inspirational keynote speech at the 2004 Democratic Convention, Americans witnessed a new image for an African American politician.

According to political reporter Benjamin Wallace-Wells, Americans encountered a new type of political character. He was black, but not quite. He spoke white, with the hand-gestures of a management consultant, but also with the oratorical flourishes of a black preacher.[16]

Supporters and critics have likened Obama's popular image to a cultural Rorschach test, a neutral persona on whom people can project their personal histories and aspirations. Obama's own stories about his family's origins reinforce his "everyman" persona.[17] In addition, Eugene Robinson, a *Washington Post* opinion columnist, characterized Obama's political image as: "the personification of both-and, a messenger who rejects 'either-or' political choices, and [one who] could move the nation beyond the cultural wars of the 1960s."[18]

Ironically, another African American who projects a somewhat similar neutral persona is Condoleezza Rice. Condoleezza Rice is the sixty-sixth United States Secretary of State, and the first African American woman and the second African American in the current Bush administration to hold the office. Rice is only the second woman (after Madeleine Albright, who served from 1997 to 2001) to serve as Secretary of State. Rice was President Bush's National Security Advisor during his first term, but before joining the Bush administration, she was Professor of Political Science at Stanford University, where she served as Provost from 1993 to 1999.[19]

Interestingly, Condoleezza Rice was born and raised in Birmingham, Alabama, and experienced firsthand the injustices of Birmingham's discriminatory laws and attitudes during the 1950s and 1960s. As Rice recalls of her parents and their peers, "they refused to allow the limits and injustices of their time to limit our horizons."[20] Rice also states that growing up during racial segregation taught her determination against adversity and the need to be "twice as good" as the majority.[21]

According to mainstream media, Rice's policies and strong diplomatic style have gained her recognition as a powerful leader. She pioneered a policy of transformational diplomacy, with a focus on democracy in the greater Middle East, and a number of other diplomatic international agreements.

However, the African American community have not been near as supportive of her views. In fact, *Washington Post* columnist Eugene Robinson asked, "How did Rice come to a worldview so radically different from that of most black Americans?"[22] In addition, *The Black Commentator* magazine described sentiments given in a speech by Rice at a black gathering as "more than strange—they were evidence of profound personal disorientation. A black woman who doesn't know how to talk to black people is of limited political use to an administration that has few black allies."[23]

Regardless of the criticism from various segments of the African American community and accolades from mainstream media, Condoleezza Rice's image is polished, straightforward, stylish, highly-educated, and mainstream. Interestingly, these are the same attributes associated with Barack Obama. It will be quite fascinating to see how their political careers as well as those of other African American politicians who share similar image characteristics continue to develop.

CONCLUSION

Surprisingly, not much has been written about the relationship of images associated with African Americans in politics. In the world of politics, image is everything as well. Not only are physical appearance (body type—slim, heavy, tall, short), physical looks (handsome or pretty), skin color (very light brown skin, light brown skin, medium brown skin, or dark brown skin) important attributes to the success or failure of an African American politician, but more importantly the cultural image that the African American politician wants to project and how it is received by potential voters, whether they are African American or not, is really the key for success.

Recently, we have seen a change in this imagery associated with many African American politicians, and it appears that it is working. Regardless of political affiliation, more African Americans are deciding to get involved in politics (locally or nationally), because they feel that they can make a difference and also represent all Americans, not just African Americans. Indeed we are witnessing a cultural revolution happening to African Americans in the world of politics.

—— CHAPTER 10 ——

GLOBAL PERSPECTIVE: HOW ARE AFRICAN AMERICAN IMAGES VIEWED BY OTHER COUNTRIES?

INTRODUCTION

Each and every day, we hear it more and more. All of us live in a global world now: What we do here in America affects other countries; what happens in other countries affects us here in America. Whether it is the state of the U. S. economy, the state of international political agendas, the pandemic effects of infectious diseases, the trends of international fashion designs, the achievements of world-class athletes in international competition, or the continual global warming phenomenon, we here in America and in our local neighborhoods are connected to the world, and the world is connected to us. Whether we want to believe it or not, it is happening now, and it is happening faster than we ever imagined!

That is why it is so much more important to start thinking about how we as African Americans are being perceived by other people around the world. For so long, we have been so focused on and self-conscious about how mainstream European Americans and mainstream media perceive us that we have failed to recognize that there is a world of other people who are curious and fascinated about how we live our lives and what type of images best reflect who we are as a people. These other people, these other countries, and these global communities are being fed all types of images about us.

So the major questions are:

1. How are African Americans perceived by other countries?
2. Are these images culturally correct representations, or are they more stereotypical images of us?

3. Where do these images about African Americans most likely originate?
4. Are African Americans concerned about how we are perceived by other countries?
5. If we are concerned, then what can we do to correct these stereotypical images?

By answering these questions, we can begin to dispel many of the myths and misconceptions that many people of other countries have about us and also challenge many of the major media outlets that are displaying and using our physical and visual images to provide a much more diverse representation of who we are as a people. In other words, make the major media conglomerates and even the few African American-owned media outlets accountable to how we are represented—simple as that!

RESEARCH STUDY

One recent study investigating how African Americans are viewed by Latino immigrants may shed some insight into how other people in other countries view African Americans. "Racial Distancing in a Southern City: Latino Immigrants' View of Black Americans" examined the attitudes of recent Latino immigrants toward African Americans in a Southern city, Durham, North Carolina.[1]

Why Durham, North Carolina? First, North Carolina has the fastest-growing Latino population in the country. It experienced an almost 500 percent increase in its Latino population, primarily immigrants from Mexico and countries of Central America, skyrocketing from 76,726 in 1990 to 378,963 in 2000.[2] Furthermore, North Carolina had the highest rate of growth in its immigrant population out of all the states in the 1990s. Additionally, Durham, like other cities of the New South, has experienced a decline or loss of industries where African Americans have traditionally found work. As a result, a substantial portion of the African American population now works in the service industry, and many (but not necessarily all) African Americans and the new Latino immigrants find themselves competing for the same jobs. Finally, from a research and data-gathering perspective, the research team stated that Durham is of a manageable size.[3]

The research study's analyses were based on the 2003 Durham Survey of Intergroup Relations (DSIR; n = 500). The sample of 500 consisted of 160 European Americans (32%), 151 African Americans (30%), 167 Latinos (35%), 6 Asians (1.2%), 12 who designated their race as Other (2.4%), and 1 respondent (0.2%) who did not indicate a racial category.

The research team's data confirmed what they had suspected—the Latino population in Durham is basically an immigrant population, primarily from Mexico. Of the Latino respondents in the sample, 93 percent were born outside of the United States. Of the 93 percent (n = 156), only about 19 percent were naturalized citizens. Although Mexicans were the largest portion of the Latino sample (63%), Latinos from Central America were the next-largest group (23%), followed by South American (5%), Puerto Rican (4%), Spanish (2%), Cuban (1%), and Other Latino (2%).[4]

Analyses of their first hypothesis indicates that the prevalence of negative stereotypes of African Americans in the Latino immigrant community is quite widespread and seems especially so when compared to the prevalence of European American stereotypes of African Americans. Along each dimension, the stereotypes of African Americans by Latinos were more negative than those of the European American respondents. McClain et al. found that 58.9 percent of the Latino immigrants reported feeling that few or almost no African Americans are hard working; approximately one-third (32.5%) of the Latino immigrant respondents reported feeling that few or almost no African Americans are easy to get along with; and slightly more than a majority (56.9%) of the Latino immigrant respondents reported feeling that few or almost no African Americans could be trusted. Interestingly, however, the more-educated Latino immigrants have significantly less negative stereotypes about African Americans.[5]

What factors influence the stereotypes that Latinos hold of African Americans? McClain et al. stated that most likely the newly arrived Latino immigrants' negative views of African Americans originated in their home countries and were reinforced, rather than reduced, by neighborhood interactions with African Americans.[6]

What is most interesting about this research team's major finding is that the study suggests that some new immigrant populations arriving in the United States have been greatly influenced by their home country's exposure to our exported media images of African Americans. As a very large percentage of our U. S. exported media images of African Americans tend to be stereotypical and limiting, it is no wonder that newly arrived immigrants, regardless of ethnicity, have stereotypical and negative views of African Americans.[7]

WEB SITE RESPONSES

Because there are very few studies investigating the central question of how African Americans are perceived or viewed in other countries, I have decided to obtain responses directly from the latest popular Web sites that share individual accounts on how we are viewed in different countries. Of course, there are all types of Web sites from which one could obtain information on practically any topic, but I wanted to find three Web sites that were frequented the most and appeared to be the most reputable. These Web sites are:

- Black Travels.com (www.blacktravels.com)
- Café De La Soul (www.cafedelasoul.com)
- Yahoo (www.yahoo.com)

First, Black Travels.com describes itself as

an interactive Web site created for the more independent-minded [African American] traveler with a desire for knowledge and adventure. All the contributors are travelers who share a common passion for travel and live by the maxim that half the enjoyment of travel is in the vital lessons we learn about ourselves along the way. The site itself uses a number of sources for its content and links to other travel sites that hopefully [the visitor] will find useful in planning [his or her] travels. But the best resource of all is the chance to meet other [African American] travelers who are the real experts that keep this site going.[8]

The Black Travels.com Web site shows a map of the world where the site visitor can click on any of the major world destinations and receive a personal account from an African American traveler (usually with their picture) who visited the particular destination. Destinations such as the following are listed:

- Canada
- Mexico
- Caribbean
- Central and South America
- Eastern Europe
- Western Europe
- Asia
- Middle East
- Australia-Pacific
- Africa

Specifically, an African American traveler near Dublin, Ireland, who had lived in Ireland for a year, decided to venture to more of the Dublin countryside. Her personal account was as follows:

Often people assumed I was African, and they were surprised—no, startled to hear my American accent when I spoke. I was then to find out that Ireland was a country saturated with images from American television and movies. Many Irish people were surprised to find that I, as they said, "spoke good English." Several Irish nationals were also taken aback to find that I came from a middle-class, two parent home. At that time the Irish media was filled with a constant diet of one-dimensional, dysfunctional, and derogatory image of Black Americans as a violence prone, undereducated, dance-obsessed people. In the smallest of town in Ireland people seemed to think that the typical life experience for an African American included violence and personal, financial, and moral chaos. Again I was to know the sting of being summed up before being known.[9]

Another African American traveler shared his experience living and traveling in Japan for seven years. His account was as follows:

Japan is a very customer-oriented society. They are very much into intricate packaging of products, services, and what not. But the culture of the society itself is so filled with ceremony that it is not surprising that extra time and care is given to even the smallest of things. . . . The attitude toward Blacks varies. First of all there are more Africans than African Americans so many have been influenced by them as much. However the American movie industry has done much to erode our credibility as intelligent people deserving of fair treatment and a great deal to promote the stereotype of a race of violent people. Sometimes the fear is evident but at times difficult to know if it is based on being Black or just a foreigner. Stereotypes are often in effect here, especially sexually and musically. But at least the stereotypes for music have created a booming field for African American musicians such as myself.[10]

Next, the Web site Café de la Soul, officially launched in 1998, describes itself as

the premier online reference for African Americans living in and traveling to Paris. [It] gives voice to the modern black Paris community and addresses the interests and needs of today's urban travelers, all the while highlighting a virtually hidden side of the city of light. Café de la Soul's mission is simple: to inspire its readers to explore a culturally significant Paris in a way they perhaps never dreamed possible.[11]

Specifically, one of the personal accounts from an African American who offers tours of historical black Paris, when asked what the French think of African Americans, is as follows:

What Do the French think of African Americans? You're right to think they have a good impression of us. . . that good impression comes from that fact that historically, the African American on French soil proved their excellence through pure talent. Namely in jazz and the influence of Josephine Baker at the beginning of the century.

On a more contemporary note, the influence of hip hop and rap has been enormous. The young French not only listened to it, they made it their own and created in the same form a very unique way of expressing themselves, that differentiated them from anything that came before. . . TV series like Cosby help to lend a positive image but there is also all that negative media that seeps out that color the French and the world's idea of what African America is like.

The French sees the African American as an oppressed, undervalued people in their own land and that seems to bring out their sheltering nature. By welcoming the African American in France, they're also mocking white America. African Americans are not perceived to have power in the U.S. so they are non-threatening. Most African Americans living in France will probably tell you they feel more at ease walking down the street in Paris than at home. And when the police come into the subway checking everybody's identification, the African American will get it just like anybody else, but the American in African American will give him/her that clout needed in such situations.[12]

Finally, the Web site Yahoo.com—one of the largest search engines on the Web—provides a section called Yahoo! Answers. The following question was asked: "How are African Americans viewed by other nations?"[13]

Members of Yahoo.com responded with their own particular personal accounts and answers. Two responses caught my attention. They were as follows:

African Americans are viewed by other nations by what they see on T.V. and usually that means in a stereotypical way. So if you see a bunch of rappers, thugs, gangsters, dead beat dads, flashy, pimpish, clown-type, dancing/jumping around, stylized African American on T.V. and that's all you know of that culture then you are going to assume that that's what and how they are. I have a half brother who lives in Australia where this not typically the case, but if you go to underdeveloped nations or nations with minimal black people (areas) Africa, India, China they don't know any "real black people" just what is on T.V...

What's disappointing (scary) is some from said nations people come to this country as immigrants and often times treat African Americans poorly due to misinformation (this sometimes is especially true with African immigrants who look down on American born Americans).[14]

Another Yahoo member responded:

African Americans are viewed by other countries/people in so many different ways. Several years ago, people's viewpoints were very much the same (racist, bias and discriminating). Now as the world has progressed, people view African Americans as strong individuals, equality has come a long way where they are recognized as the same as you and I. There are obviously a lot of people that have not changed their viewpoints and are still very racist, but in time the world will change as a whole.[15]

In general, these personal accounts from three major Web sites highlight the need to not only start thinking about how African American images are perceived globally, both physically and culturally, but they also indicate that we need to do something about these false, limiting, stereotypical views about African American culture, whether in the music, movies, entertainment, fashion, sports, fitness, television, or other industries.[16] As the personal accounts suggest, these stereotypical images have been exported to each and every one of these countries, and we (American mainstream industries) are not providing a balanced, more diverse representation for people in other countries to see or read about.

CONCLUSION

The time is now to recognize that all of us live in a global environment—a new day and age where information is shared across the world at the speed of light. The advantage with our advancing new electronic technologies is that we can see and hear what is happening in all parts of the world with just a click on our computer, a download of an image to our iPod, or the visual images on our televisions from our cable or satellite programs. So the opportunity to send or receive all types of images, no matter what part of the globe one lives in, is available to a much larger percentage of people than ever before.

Nonetheless, surprisingly, with all of these media and electronic opportunities at our fingertips, a substantial percentage of the world beyond the U.S. borders has a very limited perception of African American lifestyle and culture, let alone the type of body images and body types that we prefer. This is a fact, and there is no other way to get around it except to finally confront it, take action, and realize that we can change how the world sees us.

—— CHAPTER 11 ——

CONCLUSION

INTRODUCTION

Quite honestly, I did not realize that the issue of body image was so important to African Americans until I completed my last book, *Food Choice and Obesity in Black America: Creating a New Cultural Diet,* and started to promote it across the country.[1] After receiving so many questions and inquiries, and having many lively discussions about how the African American preferred body images and body types are so different from other groups, I began to conduct my follow-up research of the topic with a completely different approach. In my initial research, I primarily focused on just the health connection and how it is so important to an individual's well-being and ability to lose weight.

Then, I started to expand the concept of body image from strictly a health perspective to more of a social, historical, gender, age, and ethnicity perspective. By expanding this concept, I was better able to recognize the multitude of factors that were connected to not only the generic concept of body image but particularly to the African American meaning of body image.

As with all groups in America, we all adhere in varying degrees to a certain standardization of a concept such as body image. This standardization allows for a baseline of understanding and cooperation when everyone is being evaluated equally for this particular concept.

Unfortunately, many of the standardized measurements or concepts in our America are based upon Eurocentric or mainstream American ideologies and frameworks. Thus, at the core of a concept such as body image, the standardized body image is not inclusive of other people's concepts of body image, such as in the case for African Americans. Therefore, as African Americans we are judged, evaluated, and assessed by another group's standards—which is wrong!

REASON FOR WRITING THIS BOOK

One of the major reasons for writing this book is that, as a country, we need to learn how other people, groups, populations, and individuals perceive their world and how they perceive themselves. Body image is one major way to learn not only how a people perceive themselves physically, but more importantly how they perceive themselves mentally and emotionally.

As a people, we African Americans have not been given that opportunity to truly embrace our unique physicality and mental and emotional attachments to body image until now. For centuries, our body images and body types have been devalued and ridiculed in our America. Today, we African Americans are taking ownership and speaking out about our body images and body types in very positive ways.

For example, in a recent article in the magazine *Sister 2 Sister*, a columnist addressed the issue of the lack of black models in the fashion industry today.[2] Just days after the New York Fashion Week, Bethann Hardison, former fashion model, agency owner, and model manager, moderated a panel discussion with fashion industry elite. The topics were:

- Why does the fashion model of color remain a category?
- Why in the last decade are these models not getting enough exposure?[3]

Starting off the panel discussion, Bethann Hardison stated that we all know that there is a problem in the industry, and she was asking who was to blame. Noting that image-makers do not have an eye for black beauty, she specifically pointed out the following familiar scenarios:

- A typical agency only has one black top model.
- Black covers do not sell.
- Designers are not sensitive to the lack of diversity.
- Agencies hold black models back from being in black magazines.
- Black celebrities suddenly entering the world of the nouveau riche do not realize the struggles of the past and do not have a clue as to what went on before they became stars.[4]

Panelists such as designer Michael Volbrach, who spoke of his days as designer for the Bill Blass line of fashion—where he was ridiculed not only for using black models, but for using older models—and author and former model Barbara Summers (*Skin Deep: Inside the World of Black Fashion*

Models and *Black and Beautiful: How Women of Color Changed the Fashion Industry*[5]), who spoke about the impact of black fashion models twenty to forty years ago, provided excellent examples of the problems within the fashion industry. Additional commentary by Harriette Cole, creative director of *Ebony*, James Tully, a white casting agent, Ivan Bard, Senior Vice President of IMG Model Management, along with former fashion models Iman and Naomi Campbell shared additional personal stories about the continual problems that African American models have with the mainstream American fashion model industry.

In general, this panel discussion is just the beginning of an ongoing conversation about the problems with the current mainstream American fashion industry. Specifically, Bethann Hardison stated, "We have to keep on talking. This is the rumble in the jungle. It's the worst time in fashion. The fashion industry is so unsexy right now. Until the media puts their foot down, we can never move forward."[6]

POSITIVE INDICATORS OF A CULTURAL REVOLUTION CHANGING AMERICA'S BODY IMAGE STANDARDS

Ebony Fashion Fair

Fortunately, there is a major outlet for black fashion models to showcase their skills, learn the art of fashion modeling, and work in their profession—the Ebony Fashion Fair, the world's largest traveling fashion show. As stated earlier in the book, my fieldwork experience at the Ebony Fashion Fair event in Greensboro, North Carolina, was a cultural fashion event that I could never forget, but also an event in which I found a new appreciation and respect for black beauty as it relates to African American body images and body types (Bailey 11/3/2007).

Former Ebony Fashion Fair model, author, host, and commentator Jada Collins superbly provided the professional commentary to all the Glam Odyssey fashion modeled by the thirteen female and male models. The diversity of African American body types wearing all types of domestic and international high fashion outfits (women and men) and particularly the reaction from the audience (women and men) at the North Carolina A&T University auditorium helped me to truly understand the social, historical, gender, age, and cultural impact that it gives back to us during each and every show. As one of the few African American males in the audience sitting with their spouses, I realized that it also provided men in the audience positive reaffirmation for our unique body types and preferred body images. By the end of the show, it became a reaffirmation and appreciation for all of our body types, our style of production, our style of interaction, and who we are as a people—Americans of African descent.

My Black is Beautiful

Another positive indicator of a cultural revolution changing America's body image standards is the campaign sponsored by Procter & Gamble: "My Black is Beautiful," which is a celebration of African American beauty in all of its manifestations. Although conceived by Procter and Gamble, it is a national conversation hosted by African American women about how they define and promote their own beauty standards."[7]

Directed by Najoh Tita-Reid, Associate Director of Multicultural Marketing at Procter and Gamble, this initiative is to celebrate the personal and collective beauty of black women. As an African American mother of two children, Associate Director Najoh Tita-Reid hopes that her daughter grows up in an environment that welcomes her unique qualities and abilities, one that recognizes and honors her inner and outer beauty. Because so many black girls see negative images of black women in media and entertainment that define their standard of beauty, My Black is Beautiful is designed to correct those negative images and to bring black girls and women together to discuss the positive images associated with African American body types.

During the summer of 2007, Procter and Gamble introduced the My Black is Beautiful movement to the entertainment community during the BET Awards and to black journalists during the National Association of Black Journalists' annual convention. They also awarded action grants to local groups committed to empowering young girls. In 2008, they plan to conduct a national conversation that will provide a forum to celebrate our inner and outer beauty. Additionally, the My Black is Beautiful Web site, www.myblackisbeautiful.com, provides a personal journal and discussion guide for individuals so that they can personally document their beauty journey and take action, large or small, toward defining their standard of beauty for African American women of all ages.[8]

Campaign for Real Beauty

Another positive indicator of a cultural revolution changing America's body image standards is the global campaign sponsored by Dove (manufactured by Unilever North America) called "Campaign for Real Beauty." Dove launched the Campaign for Real Beauty in September 2004 with an ad campaign featuring women whose appearances are outside the stereotypical norms of beauty. The brand's commitment to inspiring positive self-image among women has extended to initiatives that support a wider definition of beauty.[9]

Tackling the topic of body image is the next progressive step in the Dove global Campaign for Real Beauty. Dove hopes to change the way women perceive their bodies and their beauty by broadening the definition of what it means to be beautiful. This new campaign initiative is intended to make more women feel beautiful every day—celebrating diversity and real women by challenging today's stereotypical view of beauty. The brand uses images of real women with real bodies and real curves to accomplish this goal.

Six brave women (three African American)—two students, a kindergarten teacher, a manicurist, an administrative assistant and a café barista—dared to bare it, facing the world in nothing but their underwear and a lot of sassy attitude. Their images have not been altered or retouched in any way. Their message: "Stand firm and celebrate your curves!"[10]

Black America Body Beautiful.com

Finally, as an applied cultural and medical anthropologist, I am an academician who not only researches and writes about cultural and health issues, but who also takes action. After recognizing how much the various industries are incorporating our physical images to promote their products (fashion, clothing, advertising, fitness, professional sports, television, movies, entertainment, political affiliations) as well as all the misinformation that so many countries have about African Americans, both physically and culturally, I have decided to start my own professional Web site.

The new Web site will be called "Black America Body Beautiful."[11] The objectives of my new Web site will be as follows:

1. To promote more accurate representations of physical and visual images of African Americans;
2. To dialogue about the types of physical and visual images associated with African Americans among African Americans and non-African Americans;
3. To encourage the fashion, clothing, fitness, television, movie, advertising, political, and entertainment industries to use more accurate and diverse representations of body types and positive images associated with African Americans as well as all underrepresented populations;
4. To mobilize concerned African Americans and non-African Americans in communicating our issues with the appropriate corporations and their leadership structures so that effective, culturally competent changes can occur;
5. To network with other countries to learn about their concerns with regards to how Americans and African Americans perceive their particular images; and
6. To become the cultural spokesperson of an organization that provides professional advice to corporations on how to accurately portray African Americans in the various industries.

It is anticipated that my Web site and the activities associated with it will also motivate other concerned individuals of other ethnicities to take action so that all of us can be better represented physically and culturally.

CONCLUSION

It is truly amazing to me that this book's topic focusing on body image symbolizes what was wrong with America in the past and now what is still wrong with America in the present. My parents and teachers always taught me that America is a country that values freedom, rewards hard work, and encourages diversity. Today, more than ever, America is supposed to be a country where you can be what you want to be and express your views and thoughts, because that is your right as a U.S. citizen. Yet for some reason, this issue of body image and body types, particularly as it relates to African Americans, has been purposefully neglected and overlooked for years.

It is quite apparent that our mainstream American society wants all of us to adhere to the same standards on just about everything. The method by which various industries operate and strategically coerce a majority of Americans into looking a certain way, buying a certain product, and accepting a certain standard of beauty is disturbing. It is as though the average American is not allowed to have a mind of his or her own. That is what is wrong with America!

Then, what happens when a large segment of Americans such as African Americans do not believe that they have to look a certain way, do not buy certain mainstream products, and do not accept a certain standard of beauty? They create their own system that is separate from mainstream American society. That is exactly what African Americans have decided to do.

We created our own system and standards of beauty such as Madame C. J. Walker hair and beauty products during the early 1900s. That is why we created our own fashion shows such as the Ebony Fashion Fair International Traveling Fashion Show, celebrating its fiftieth anniversary. That is why we created our own black film industry (i.e., Black Hollywood) and television networks such Black Entertainment Network (B.E.T) and TV One. That is why we created our own competitive sports leagues such as the Negro Baseball leagues from the 1920s to 1940s and all the competitive sports associated with the historically black colleges and universities (HBCUs). That is why we created our own coalitions within the American political system. Finally, that is why we continue to create new sites on the Web to highlight issues specific to African Americans. Although these systems and standards varied depending upon what part of the country a person lived, African Americans took pride and are still taking pride in not only creating something for themselves, but also maintaining it so that they can have something of their own and be rewarded for their efforts.

That is also the reason why so many African Americans became success-ful entrepreneurs in businesses related to beauty, fashion, advertising, fit-ness, entertainment, and politics. Thus if it were not for this separate system established within most African American communities in America, we would not have established our preferred standards of beauty, fashion, entertainment and competitive sports.

That is one of the ironic twists to this dual world system in which African Americans have had to live. On one hand, we are completely ignored, ridiculed, stereotyped, not accepted, and not acknowledged for our beauty, fashion, fitness, politics, and entertainment achievements, but on the other hand, it motivated us to establish our own beauty standards, fashion stan-dards, political agendas, entertainment standards, and competitive sports standards.

Yet another ironic twist has occurred. The standards that we have estab-lished for beauty, fashion entertainment, competitive sports, politics, and particularly body image are now dramatically influencing mainstream America's standards of beauty, fashion, politics, competitive sports, and, of course, preferred body images. Even mainstream American society is finally challenging the strict guidelines and standards for what they consider an ideal body type or ideal beauty. They are finally realizing that their strict guidelines associated with ideal body type and ideal beauty have caused tremendous psychological and medical problems (e.g., chronic obsessive behaviors, anorexia, and bulimia) to many young girls and women in America.

Fortunately, a number of major corporations in advertising, fashion, fit-ness, and entertainment (television and movies) have recognized this cul-tural revolution for a new standard of preferred body images, body types, beauty, entertainment, and physical fitness. Although many of these cor-porations were ridiculed initially for taking a chance with the African American population in major industry endeavors, primarily because they perceived there was not enough profit to be made, now they are consid-ered pioneers and leaders in their respective industries. That is what is right with America!

Yet with all of the changes that have occurred and that will continue to occur in America within the beauty, fashion, advertising, fitness, political, and entertainment fields, I am reminded of the profound words and philos-ophy of W.E.B. Du Bois, the first African American to receive a Ph.D. from Harvard University (1895); in his book, *The Souls of Black Folk,* he writes the following:

The Negro is a sort of seventh son, born with a veil, and gifted with second-sight in this American world—a world which yields him no true self-consciousness, but only lets him see himself through the revelation of the other world. It is a peculiar sensation, this double-consciousness, but only lets him see himself through the revelation of the other world. It is a peculiar sensation, this double-consciousness, this sense of always looking at one's self through the eyes of others, of measuring one's soul by the tape of a world that looks on in amused contempt and pity. One ever feels his two-ness—an American, a Negro, two souls, two thoughts, two unreconciled strivings; two warring ideals in one dark body, whose dogged strength alone keeps it from being torn asunder.[12]

This two-ness, this double-consciousness, and this double lifestyle in which many African Americans continue to live has brought about this cultural revolution for a new set of preferred body images and body types—not only to mainstream America but also to the world.

NOTES

CHAPTER 1

1. *BusinessWeek Online*, "Brand New Day: Thoughts on Marketing and Advertising" (2005).

2. *Thirdage Blog*, "Nike—Go Sit in the Corner" (2006), http://blog.thirdage.com/?p=126.

3. *Apple Bottom Jeans* (2007), http://www.applebottoms.com/company.asp.

4. *Oprah.com*, "Oprah's Favorite Things: Holiday 2004" (2004), www.oprah.com.

5. *Spiegel Catalogue Shape Fx* (2006), "Introducing Our New Curvy-Fit Push-Up Jeans."

6. Barbara Summers, *Black and Beautiful: How Women of Color Changed the Fashion Industry*. New York: Amistad, 2001.

7. *People Magazine* (2007) "Tyra Talks." February 5, 82–88.

8. David Heber, *The L. A. Shape Diet: The 14-Day Total Weight-Loss Plan*. New York: Regan Books, 2004.

9. *Diet Blog* (2006), http://www.diet-blog.com/archives/2006/05/01/unemployment_better_than_fat.php

CHAPTER 2

1. J. M. Last. *A Dictionary of Epidemiology* (2nd ed.) New York: Oxford University Press, 1988.

2. R. King and W. Stansfield. *A Dictionary of Genetics*. New York: Oxford University Press, 1990

3. E. Becker and S. Landav. *International Dictionary of Modern and Biology*. New York: Oxford University Press, 1986.

4. P. Brown and M. Konner (1987). "An anthropological perspective on obesity." *Annals of the New York Academy of Sciences* 499: 29–46; J. Stevens, S. Kumanyika, and J. Keil (1994). "Attitudes toward body size and dieting: differences between elderly black and white women." *American Journal of Public Health* 84: 1322–1325; J. Dounchis, H. Hayden, and D. Wilfley (2001). "Obesity, body image and eating disorders in ethnically diverse children and adolescents." In K. Thompson and L. Smolak (Eds.), *Body Image, Eating Disorders and Obesity in Youth*. Washington, DC: American Psychological Association, 67–90; L. Smolak, and M. Levine (2001). "Body image in children." In K. Thompson and L. Smolak (Eds.), *Body Image, Eating Disorders and Obesity in Youth*. Washington, DC: American Psychological Association, 41–66; S. Gore 1999. "African American women's perceptions of weight. Paradigm shift for advanced practice." *Holistic Nursing Practice* 13: 71–79; K. Pulvers, R. Lee, H. Kaur, M.Mayo, M. Flitzgibbon, S. Jeffries, J. Butler, Q. Hou, and J. Ahluwalia (2004). "Development of a culturally relevant body image instrument among urban African Americans." *Obesity Research* 12(10): 1641–1651.

5. F. Cachelin, R. Rebeck, G. Chung, and E. Pelayo (2002), "Does Ethnicity Influence Body Size Preference? A Comparison of Body Image and Body Size," *Obesity Research* 6: 62–68.

6. L. Parker (2007). "Student Perspective on Radio Racial Epithet," *The North Carolina A&T Register* 80(22): 2.

7. B. Carter and J. Steinberg (2007). "Off the Air: The Light Goes Out for Don Imus." *New York Times*. April 13th.

8. Ibid., 2

9. Sarah Grogan, *Body Image: Understanding Body Dissatisfaction in Men, Women and Children*. London: Routledge, 1999.

10. E. Bailey, *Medical Anthropology and African American Health*. Westport, CT: Bergin & Garvey, 2002.

11. E. Bailey, *Food Choice and Obesity in Black America: Creating a New Cultural Diet*. Westport, CT: Praeger Publishers, 2006, 108.

12. Thomas LaVeist. *Minority Populations and Health: An Introduction to Health Disparities in the United States*. San Francisco: Jossey-Bass, 2005, 25.

13. Ibid., 26.

14. Grogan, *Body Image*.

15. A. Fallon, "Culture in the Mirror: Sociocultural Determinants of Body Image," in *Body Images: Development, Deviance and Change* (T. Cash and T. Pruzinsky, Eds.). New York: Guilford Press, 1990, 80–109.

16. Grogan, *Body Image*.

17. R. Gordon, *Anorexia and Bulimia: Anatomy of a Social Epidemic*. Oxford: Blackwell, 1990.

18. Grogan, *Body Image*, 14

19. Ibid.

20. A. Mazur (1986). "U. S. Trends in Feminine Beauty and Overadaptation." *Journal of Sex Research*. 22: 281–303.

21. Grogan, *Body Image*.

22. Ibid.

23. Thomas Cash and Thomas Pruzinsky, "Understanding Body Images: Historical and Contemporary Perspectives," In *Body Image: A Handbook of*

Theory, Research and Clinical Practice (T. Cash and T. Pruzinsky, Eds.). New York: The Guilford Press, 2002, 18.

24. Grogan, *Body Image,* 16

25. Ibid.

26. K. Grover, "Fitness in American Culture: Images of Health, Sport, and the Body," 1830–1940." Amherst, MA: The University of Massachusetts Press, 1989, 14.

27. Ibid., 37.

28. Grogan, *Body Image,* 17.

29. T. LaVeist. *Minority Populations and Health.* San Francisco, CA: Jossey-Bass, 2005.

30. *Latin American Wave.* (1997). "What is an Hispanic?" Indianapolis: October. Page 6.

31. A. Vazquez and A. Krodel. *America's Hispanic Heritage: An Overview of Hispanics in the United States.* Ann Arbor: University of Michigan Press, 1989: 2.

32. LaVeist, *Minority Populations and Health.*

33. A. J. Ericksen, C. Markey, and B. Tinsley, "Familial Influences on Mexican American and Euro-American Preadolescent Boys' and Girls' Body Dissatisfaction," *Eating Behaviors* 4 (2003): 245–255; R. Garner, B. Friedman, and N. Jackson, "Hispanic and White Children Children's Judgments of Perceived and Ideal Body Size in Self and Others," *Psychological Record* 49 (1999): 555–564. D. Barry and C. Grilo, "Eating and Body Image Disturbances in Adolescent Psychiatric Inpatients: Gender and Ethnicity Patterns," *International Journal of Eating Disorders* 32 (2002): 335–343; T. Nieri, S. Kulis, V. Keith, and D. Hurdle, "Body Image, Acculturation, and Substance Abuse among Boys and Girls in the Southwest," *American Journal of Drug and Alcohol Abuse* 31 (2005): 617–639; J. Smith and J. Krejci, "Minorities Join the Majority: Eating Disturbances among Hispanic and Native American Youth," *International Journal of Eating Disorders* 10 (1991): 179–186; M. Story, S. French, M. Resnick, and R. Blum, "Ethnic/Racial and Socio-economic Differences in Dieting Behaviors and Body Image Perceptions in Adolescents," *International Journal of Eating Disorders* 18 (1995): 173–179; M. Serdula, M. Collins, D. Williamson et al., "Weight Control Practices of U. S. Adolescents and Adults," *Annals of Internal Medicine* 119 (1993): 667–671; F. Cachelin, Rebeck, Chung, and Pelayo, "Does Ethnicity Influence Body Size Preference?," 62–68; J. Demarest and R. Allen, "Body Image: Gender, Ethnic, and Age Differences," *Journal of Social Psychology* 140 (2000): 465–472; K. Miller, D. Gleaves, T. Hirsch, et al., "Comparisons of Body Image Dimensions by Race/Ethnicity and Gender in a University Population," *International Journal of Eating Disorders* 27 (2000): 310–316; S. Paeratakul, M. White, D. Williamson, D. Ryan, and G. Bray, "Sex, Race/Ethnicity, Socioeconomic Status, and BMI in Relation to Self-Perception of Overweight," *Obesity Research* 10 (2001): 345–350.

34. Madeline Altabe, "Ethnicity and Body Image: Quantitative and Qualitative Analysis," *International Journal of Eating Disorders* 23 (1998): 153–159

35. Cash and Pruzinsky, "Understanding Body Images," 3–12.

36. L. Ricciardelli, M. McCabe, R. Williams, and J. Thompson, "The Role of Ethnicity and Culture in Body Image and Disordered Eating among Males," *Clinical Psychology Review* 27 (2007): 582–606.

37. P. Min. *Asian Americans: Contemporary Trends and Issues.* Thousand Oaks, CA: Sage, 1995.

38. E. Bailey. Medical Anthropology and African American Health. Westport, CT: Bergin & Garvey, 2002.

39. T. Cash and T. Pruzinsky (Eds.). *Body Images, Development, Deviance and Change.* New York: Guilford Press, 1990.

40. P. Craig, V. Halavatau, E. Comino, and I. Caterson, "Perception of Body Size in the Tongan Community: Differences from and Similarities to an Australian sample," *International Journal of Obesity* 23 (1999): 1288–1294; P. Craig, B. Swinburn, T. Matenga-Smith, H. Matangi, and G. Vaughan, "Do Polynesians Still Believe that Big is Beautiful? Comparison of Body Size Perceptions and Preferences of Cook Islands, Maori, and Australians," *New Zealand Medical Journal* 109 (1996): 200–203; A. Yates, J. Edman, and M. Aruguete, "Ethnic Differences in BMI and Body/Self Dissatisfaction among Whites, Asian Subgroups, Pacific Islanders, and African Americans," *Journal of Adolescent Health* 34 (2004): 300–307.

41. P. Metcalf, R. Scragg, P. Willoughby, S. Finau, and D. Tipene-Leach, "Ethnic Differences in Perceptions of Body Size in Middle-Aged European, Maori and Pacific People Living in New Zealand," *International Journal of Obesity* 24 (2000): 593–599.

42. A. Becker, R. Burwell, S. Gilman, D. Herzog, and P. Hamburg, "Eating Behaviors Following Prolonged Exposure to Television among Ethnic Fijian Adolescent Girls," *British Journal of Psychiatry* 180 (2002): 509–514; Ricciardelli, McCabe, Williams, and Thompson, "The Role of Ethnicity and Culture," 597.

43. Cash and Pruzinsky, "Understanding Body Images," 245.

44. T. Robinson, J. Chang, K. Haydel, and J. Killen, "Overweight Concerns and Body Dissatisfaction among Third-Grade Children: The Impacts of Ethnicity and Socio-economic Status," *Journal of Pediatrics* 138 (2001): 181–187; S. Ahmad, G. Waller, and C. Verduyn, "Eating Attitudes and Body Satisfaction among Asian and Caucasian Adolescents," *Journal of Adolescence* 17 (1994): 461–470; Kowner, R. 2002 Japanese Boy Image: Structure and Esteem Scores in a Cross-Cultural Perspective. *International Journal of Psychology* 37: 149–159.; Lerner, R., Iwawaki, S., Chihara, T., and Sorell, G. 1980. Self-Concept, Self-Esteem, and Body Attitudes among Japanese Male and Female Adolescents. *Child Development* 51: 847–855; D. Neumark-Sztainer, J. Croll, M. Story, , P. Hannan, S. French, and C. Perry, "Ethnic/racial Differences in Weigh-Related Concerns and Behaviors among Adolescent Girls and Boys: Findings from Project EAT," *Journal of Psychosomatic Research* 52 (2002): 963–974; J. Edman and A. Yates, "A Cross-cultural Study of Disordered Eating Attitudes among Filipino and Caucasian Americans," *Eating Disorders: The Journal of Treatment and Prevention,* 13 (2005): 279–289; J. Sjostedt, J. Schumaker, and S. Nathawatt, "Eating Disorders among Indian and Australian University Students," *Journal of Social Psychology* (2001): 351–357; Yates, Edman, and Aruguete, "Ethnic Differences in BMI"; Story, French, Resnick, and Blum, "Ethnic/Racial and Socio-economic Differences"; Cachelin, R. Rebeck, G. Chung, and E. Pelayo, "Does Ethnicity Influence Body-Size Preference? A Comparison of Body Image and Body Size." *Obesity Research* 10: 158–166; Altabe, "Ethnicity and Body Image"; Chi-Fu Yang, P. Gray, and H. Pope, "Male Body Image in Taiwan Versus the West: *Yanggang Zhiqi* Meets the Adonis Complex," *American Journal of Psychiatry* 162 (2005): 263–269.

45. Yang, Gray, and Pope, "Male Body Image in Taiwan."

46. Yang, C., Gray, P., and Pope, H. 2002. "Male Body Image in Taiwan Versus the West, Yanggang Ahiqui Meets the Adonis Complex" *American Journal of Psychiatry* 162: 2: 263–269.: 263.

47. Yang, Gray, and Pope, "Male Body Image in Taiwan," 265.

48. Ibid., 266

49. Ibid., 267

50. T. Cash and T. Pruzinsky (Eds.). *Body Images, Development, Deviance and Change.* New York: Guilford Press, 1990.

51. Neumark-Sztainer, Croll, Story, et al., "Ethnic/Racial Differences in Weight-Related Concerns"; Smith and Krejci, "Minorities Join the Majority"; Story, French, Resnick, and Blum, "Ethnic/Racial and Socio-economic Differences."

52. Neumark-Sztainer, Croll, Story, et al., "Ethnic/Racial Differences in Weight-Related Concerns"; Story, French, Resnick, and Blum, "Ethnic/Racial and Socio-economic Differences."

53. I. Ring and D. Firman 1998. "Reducing Indigenous Mortality in Australia: Lessons from Other Countries." *Medical Journal of Australia.* 169: 528–533.

54. Ricciardelli, McCabe, Williams, and Thompson, "The Role of Ethnicity and Culture," 597.

CHAPTER 3

1. T. Cochran, *Podcasting: The Do-It Yourself Guide.* Indianapolis, IN: Wiley Publishing, Inc., 2005.

2. E. Bailey, *Food Choice and Obesity in Black America.* Westport, CT: Praeger, 2006: 44–45.

3. Ibid., 49.

4. T. Robinson, J. Chang, K. Haydel, and J. Killen. "Overweight concerns and body dissatisfaction among third-grade children: The impacts of ethnicity and socioeconomic status," *Journal of Pediatrics* 138 (2002): 181–187.

5. Ibid.

6. Ibid., 184.

7. Ibid.

8. Ibid., 186.

9. S. Thompson, S. Corwin, and R. Sargent. "Ideal body size beliefs and weight concerns of fourth-grade children," *International Journal of Eating Disorders* 21(2001): 279–284.

10. Ibid., 283.

11. Ibid., 284.

12. C. Welch, S.Gross, Y. Bronner, D. Dewberry-Moore, and D. Paige. "Discrepancies in body image perception among fourth-grade public school children from urban, suburban, and rural Maryland," *Journal of the American Dietic Association* 1040 (2004): 1080–1085.

13. Ibid., 1081.

14. Ibid., 1082.

15. Ibid., 1084.

16. Ibid.

17. S. Parker, M. Nichter, M. Nichter, S. C. Vuckovic, and C. Ritenbaugh. "Body image and weight concerns among African American and white adolescent

females: Differences that make a difference," *Human Organization* 54 (1995): 103–114.

18. Ibid., 105.

19. Ibid.

20. Ibid., 108.

21. Ibid.

22. Ibid.

23. Ibid.

24. Ibid.

25. Ibid.

26. M. Altabe, "Ethnicity and Body Image: Quantitative and Qualitative Analysis," *International Journal of Eating Disorders* 23 (1998): 155.

27. Ibid., 157.

28. Ibid., 158.

29. K. Miller, D. Gleaves, T. Hirsch, B. Green, A. Snow, and C. Corbett. "Comparisons of body image dimensions by race/ethnicity and gender in a university population," *International Journal of Eating Disorders* 27 (2000): 310–316.

30. Ibid., 312.

31. Ibid., 314–315.

32. Ibid., 315.

33. F. Cachelin et al., "Does Ethnicity Influence Body-Size Preference? A Comparison of Body Image and Body Size," *Obesity Research* 10 (2002): 160.

34. Ibid., 158–166.

35. Ibid., 165.

36. D. Becker et al., "Body Image Preferences among Urban African Americans and Whites from Low-income Communities," *Ethnicity & Disease* 9 (1999): 377–386.

37. Ibid., 381.

38. K. Pulvers, R. Lee, H. Kaur, M. Mayo, M. Flitzgibbon, Sl Jeffries, J. Butler, Q. Hou, and J. Ahluwalia. "Development of a culturally relevant body image instrument among urban African Americans," *Obesity Research* 12(10): 1641–1651.

39. P. Brown and M. Konner, "An Anthropological Perspective on Obesity," *Annals of the New York Academy of Sciences* 499 (1987): 29–46; J. Stevens, S. Kumanyika, and J. Keil. "Attitudes toward body size and dieting: Differences between elderly black and white women." *American Journal of Public Health* 84 (1994): 1322–1325. J. Dounchis, H. Hayden, and D. Wilfley. "Obesity, body image and eating disorders in ethnically diverse children and adolescents," In *Body Image, Eating Disorders and Obesity in Youth,* K. Thompson and L. Smolak (Eds.). Washington, DC: American Psychological Association, 2001: 67–80; L. Smolak, and M. Levine, "Body image in children," in *Body Image, Eating Disorders and Obesity in Youth,* K. Thompson and K. Smolack (Eds.). Washington, DC: American Psychological Association, 2001: 41–66; S. Gore, "African American women's perceptions of weight: Paradigm shift for advanced practice," *Holistic Nursing Practices* 13 (1999): 71–79; K. Pulvers, R. Lee, H. Kaur, M. Mayo, M. Flitzgibbon, Sl Jeffries, J. Butler, Q. Hou, and J. Ahluwalia, "Development of a culturally relevant body image instrument among urban African Americans," *Obesity Research* 12(10) (2004)

40. M. Baskin, H. Ahluwalia, and K. Resnicow, "Obesity Intervention among African American Children and Adolescents," *Pediatric Clinics of North America* 48 (2001): 1036.

CHAPTER 4

1. Thomas LaVeist, *Minority Populations and Health: An Introduction to Health Disparities in the United States*. San Francisco, CA: Jossey-Bass, 2005: 1.

2. Michael Harris, *Colored Pictures: Race and Visual Representation*. Chapel Hill, NC: University of North Carolina Press, 2003: 2.

3. Ibid., 3.

4. Ibid., 9.

5. Ibid., 14.

6. Ibid., 15.

7. Ibid., 32.

8. Ibid., 40.

9. Ibid., 44.

10. Ibid., 40.

11. Ibid., 63.

12. Ibid.

13. Ibid., 88.

14. Ibid.

15. Ibid., 90.

16. Joseph White and James Cones, III, *Black Men Emerging: Facing the Past and Seizing a Future in America*. New York: W. H. Freeman and Company, 1999: 22.

17. Ibid., 23.

18. Ibid., 27.

19. John Blassingame, *The Slave Community*. New York: Oxford University Press, 1979.

20. Ibid., 225.

21. White and Cones, III, *Black Men Emerging* (1999), 35.

22. Ibid., 37.

23. Paul Mullins, *Race and Affluence: An Archaeology of African America and Consumer Culture*. New York: Kluwer Academic, 1999: 64.

24. Shane White and Graham White, *Stylin': African American Expressive Culture from Its Beginnings to the Zoot Suit*. Ithaca, NY: Cornell University Press, 1998, 41.

25. Ibid., 47.

26. Ibid., 54.

27. Maxine Craig, *Ain't I a Beauty Queen? Black Women, Beauty, and the Politics of Race*. Oxford: Oxford University Press, 2002, 34.

28. A'Lelia Bundles, *On Her Own: The Life and Times of Madam C. J. Walker*. New York: Washington Square Press, 2001, 25.

29. Ibid., 43.

30. Ibid., 40.

31. Ibid., 44.

32. Ibid., 63.
33. Ibid.
34. Ibid., 60.
35. Noliwe Rooks, *Hair Raising: Beauty, Culture, and African American Women.* New Brunswick, NJ: Rutgers University Press, 1996: 60.
36. Ibid.
37. Ibid., 64.
38. Ibid., 49.
39. Craig, *Ain't I a Beauty Queen?*, 34.
40. Rooks, *Hair Raising*, 136.
41. Craig, *Ain't I a Beauty Queen?*, 46–47.
42. Ibid., 47.
43. Ibid.
44. Ibid., 48.
45. Ibid., 50.
46. Ibid.
47. Ibid., 51.
48. Ibid., 53.
49. Ibid., 56.
50. Ibid., 64.
51. Ibid.

CHAPTER 5

1. William Morris (ed.). *The American Heritage Dictionary of the English Language.* Boston: Houghton Mifflin Company, 1976: 477.
2. Barbara Summers, *Black and Beautiful: How Women of Color Changed the Fashion Industry.* New York: Amistad, 2001.
3. Ibid. xv.
4. Shane White and Graham White, *Stylin': African American Expressive Culture from Its Beginnings to the Zoot Suit.* Ithaca, NY: Cornell University Press, 1998: 205.
5. Ibid., 207.
6. Ibid., 208.
7. *Half-Century Magazine.* "Chicago's Fashion Show," March-April 1924.
8. *Pittsburgh Courier.* April 24, 1926.
9. White and White, *Stylin'*, 209.
10. Ibid., 210.
11. Ibid., 212.
12. Ibid., 213.
13. Ibid., 213.
14. Ibid., 218.
15. Ibid., 218.
16. Rosemary Miller, *Threads of Time, The Fabric of History: Profiles Of African American Dressmakers and Designers, 1850–2002.* Washington, DC: T & S Press, 2006: 5.
17. Summers, *Black*, 3.
18. Ibid., 3.

19. Ibid., 4.

20. Ibid., 4.

21. Ibid., 4.

22. Charlene Dash, in Barbara Summers, *Black and Beautiful: How Women of Color Changed the Fashion Industry*. New York: Amistad, 2001: 4.

23. Ibid., 4–5.

24. Ibid., 49.

25. Ibid., 50.

26. Ibid., 52.

27. Ibid., 64–65.

28. Ibid., 72–149.

29. Ibid., 174.

30. Keith Reed, "The Fickle Business of Fashion: According to Tyra, Iman, Kimora and Alek." *Ebony Magazine* (2007). September: 66.

31. Wikipedia.org (2007). http://en.wikipedia.org/wiki/Kimora_Lee_Simmons.

32. Kimora Lee Simmons, *Fabulosity: What It Is and How To Get It*. New York: Harper Collins Publishers, 2006: 8

33. Ibid., 176.

34. Ibid., 183.

35. Wikipedia.org (2007). http://en.wikipedia.org/wiki/Tracee_Ellis_Ross.

36. Tracee Ellis Ross, "My Tush," in *Naked: Black Women Bare All About Their Skin, Hair, Hips, Lips, and Other Parts,* Ayana Byrd and Akiba Solomon (Eds.). New York: The Berkley Publishing Group, 2005: 192.

37. Margena A. Christian, "History," *Glam Odyssey 2007–2008,* www.ebony-fashionfair.com/assembled/history.html.

38. Ibid.

39. Lynn Norment, "Defining Fabulous: Celebrating 50 Years of the Ebony Fashion Fair," *Ebony Fashion Fair Magazine*. Chicago: A Johnson Publication, Fall 2007: 110–115.

40. Christian, "History."

41. Staci Jackson quote in Lynn Norment, "Defining Fabulous: Celebrating 50 Years of the Ebony Fashion Fair," *Ebony Fashion Fair Magazine*. Chicago. A Johnson Publication, Fall 2007: 115.

CHAPTER 6

1. Jannette Dates and William Barlow, *Split Image: African Americans in the Mass Media,* 2nd ed. Washington, DC: Howard University Press, 1993, 3.

2. Ibid., 4.

3. Ibid., 5.

4. T. W. Adorno, "Television and Patterns of Mass Culture," in *Mass Culture: The Popular Arts in America*, Bernard Rosenburg and David Manning White (Eds.). New York: Free Press, 1957: 484.

5. Margery S. Berube (Ed.), "Advertising," *American Heritage Dictionary*. Boston: Houghton Mifflin Company, 1976.

6. Dates and Barlow, *Split Image,* 463.

7. Ibid., 463.

8. Ibid., 464.

9. *Magazine Publishers of America.* "African American Market Profile" (2001), http//www.magazine.org.org/marketprofiles.

10. Ibid., 14.

11. Dates and Barlow, *Split Image,* 461.

12. Home Depot Advertising Flyer, May 2007.

13. Dates and Barlow, *Split Image,* 475.

14. Ibid., 475.

15. Ibid., 478.

16. Shirley Henderson, "Mo'Nique Charms the World," *Ebony Magazine.* August (2007): 64–69.

17. Wikipedia.org, 2007, http://en.wikipedia.org/wiki/Raven-Symon%C3%A9.

18. Raven Symone Web site, 2007, http://www.raven-symone.org/press/2007/Raven%20Symone20%Ebony%2003-01-2007.php.

19. "Queen Latifah," http://en.wikipedia.org/wiki/Queen_Latifah.

20. Ibid.

21. Lynn Norment. "Queen Latifah on a Roll," *Ebony Magazine* October (2007): 86.

22. Ibid., 90.

23. "Oprah Winfrey," http://en.wikipedia.org/wiki/Oprah_Winfrey.

24 Patricia Sellers, "The Business of Being Oprah," *Fortune Magazine* May 6 (2002): 50–64.

25. Ibid., 54.

26. Ibid., 52.

Chapter 7

1. M. Nies, M. Vollman, and T. Cook, "African American Women's Experience with Physical Activity in Their Daily Lives," *Public Health Nursing* 16 (1999): 27.

2. Charlotte Pratt and Cornelius Pratt, "Nutrition advertisements in Consumer Magazines: Health Implications for African Americans," *Journal of Black Studies* 26 (1996): 504–523.

3. Brown, Lee and Vance Ferrigno, *Training for Speed, Agility, and Quickness.* Champaign: Human Kinetics, 2005.

4. Michael Boyle, *Functional Training for Sports.* Champaign: Human Kinetics, 2004.

5. Everett Aaberg, *Muscle Mechanics.* Champaign: Human Kinetics Publishers, 2006.

6. David Herber, *The L.A. Shape Diet: The 14-Day Total Weight Loss Plan.* New York: Harper Collins Publishers, 2004.

7. Ibid., inside front dust jacket flap.

8. Ibid., 43.

9. www.curves.com.

10. www.ballyfitness.com.

11. Billy Blanks, http://www.billyblanks.com, 2007.

12. R. Weaver, F. Gaines, and A. Ebron, *Slim Down Sister: The African American Women's Guide to Healthy, Permanent Weight Loss.* New York: Dutton Group, 2000.

13. Ibid., 4.

14. MaDonna Grimes, *Work It Out: The Black Women's Guide to Getting the Body You Always Wanted*. New York: Penguin Putnam, 2003.

15. Ibid., 1.

16. Ibid., 3.

17. Ibid., 63.

18. Ibid., 63–64.

19. Ibid., 126.

20. "Venus Williams" (2007), http://en.wikipedia.org/wiki/Venus_Williams.

21. David Wiggins and Patrick Miller, *The Unlevel Playing Field: A Documentary History of the African American Experience in Sport*. Chicago: University of Illinois Press, 2003.

22. "Venus Williams," http://en.wikipedia.org/wiki/Venus Williams.

23. "Serena Willilams" http://en.wikipedia.org/wiki/Serena_Williams.

24. "Serena Williams," http:// en.wikipedia.org/wiki/Serena_Williams.

25. Roy Johnson, "Sister Slam," *Savoy* (2002): 53–54, www.savoymag.com.

26. "Tiger Woods," http://en.wikipedia.org/wiki/Tiger_Woods.

27. Ibid.

28. Ibid., 12.

29. Ibid., 13.

30. Earl Woods, *Training a Tiger: A Father's Guide to Raising a Winner in Both Golf and Life*. New York: Harper Collins, 1997, 183–184.

31. Under Armour Web site, www.underarmour.com

32. Shawn Donnelly, "How Ben Got Big," *Muscle & Fitness*, December (2006): 144–154.

33. Ibid., 152.

CHAPTER 8

1. Darnell Hunt, "Making Sense of Blackness on Television," in *Channeling Blackness: Studies on Television and Race in America*, ed. by Darnell Hunt. New York: Oxford University Press, 2005: 1–24.

2. Ibid., 1.

3. Ibid., 11.

4. Ibid., 12.

5. Ibid.

6. Ibid., 270.

7. Ibid.

8. Ibid.

9. Herman Gray, "The Politics of Representation in Network Television," in *Channeling Blackness: Studies on Television and Race in America*, Darnell Hunt (Ed.). New York: Oxford University Press, 2005: 160.

10. Ibid., 161.

11. Hunt, "Making Sense," 13.

12. Ibid, 271.

13. Ibid, 273–274.

14. Beretta Smith-Shomade, *Shaded Lives: African American Women and Television*. New Brunswick, NJ: Rutgers University Press, 2002: 43.

15. Rana Emerson, "'Where My Girls At?' Negotiating Black Womanhood in Music Videos." in *Channeling Blackness: Studies on Television and Race in America*, Darnell Hunt (Ed.). New York: Oxford University Press, 2005: 212.

16. Ibid., 213.

17. Dionne Stephens and April Few, "The Effects of Images of African American Women in Hip-Hop on Early Adolescents' Attitudes Toward Physical Attractiveness and Interpersonal Relationships," *Sex Roles* 56 (2007): 251–264.

18. D. Stephens and L. Phillips, "Freaks, Gold Diggers, Divas, and Dykes: The Sociohistorical Development of African American Female Adolescent Scripts," *Sexuality and Culture* 7 (2005): 3–47.

19. Stephens and Few, "Effects," 252.

20. Ibid., 253.

21. Ibid., 254.

22. P. Bell-Scott, *Flat Footed Truths: Telling Black Women's Lives.* (New York: Henry Holt, 1998); and A. Few, D. Stephens, and M. Rouse-Arnett, "Sister-to-Sister Talk: Transcending Boundaries in Qualitative Research with Black Women," *Family Relations* 52 (2003): 205–215.

23. Stephens and Few, "Effects," 254.

24. Ibid.

25. Ibid.

26. Ibid.

27. Ibid., 254.

28. Ibid., 255.

29. Ibid.

30. Ibid.

31. Ibid.

32. Ibid.

33. Ibid.

34. Ibid., 256.

35. Ibid.

36. Ibid.

37. Ibid., 257.

38. Ibid.

39. Ibid.

40. Ibid., 258.

41. Ibid., 259.

42. B. Arogundade, *Black Beauty: A History and Celebration.* New York: Thunder's Mouth, 2000; D. Willis and C. Williams. *The Black Female Body: A Photographic History.* Philadelphia: Temple University Press, 2002.

43. Stephens and Few, "Effects," 258.

44. Ibid., 259.

45. G. Henriques, L. G. Calhoun, and A. Cann, "Ethnic Differences in Women's Body Satisfaction: An Experimental Investigation," *Journal of Social Psychology* 136 (1996): 689–698; S. Parker, M. Nichter, M. Nichter, N. Vuckovic, C. Sims, and C. Rittenbaugh, "Body Image and Weight Concerns among African American and White Adolescent Females: Differences That Make a Difference," *Human Organization* 54 (1995): 103–113; C. S. Rand and J. M. Kuldau, "Epidemiology of Bulimia and Symptoms in a General Population: Sex, Age, Race, and

Socioeconomic Status," *International Journal of Eating Disorders* 11 (1992): 37–44.

46. Stephens and Few, "Effects," 259.

47. Ibid., 259.

48. Jannette Dates and William Barlow, *Split Image: African Americans in the Mass Media.* Washington, DC: Howard University Press, 1993, 132.

49. Ibid., 132.

50. Karen Ross, *Black and White Media: Black Images in Popular Film and Television.* Cambridge: Blackwell Publishers, Inc., 1996: 57.

51. Ibid., 57.

52. Ibid., 58.

53. Ibid.

54. Ibid., 61.

55. Henry Sampson, *Blacks in Black and White: A Source Book on Black Films.* New Jersey: Scarecrow Press, 1977.

56. "Hattie McDaniel," http://en.wikipedia.org/wiki/Hattie_McDaniel.

57. Barbara Summers, *Skin Deep: Inside the World of Black Fashion Models* (New York: Amistad, 1999), 11.

58. Ross, "Black and White Media," 67.

59. "American Gangster Tops the Box Office; Denzel Washington Scores Career Best," Black Talent News, http://www.blacktalentnews.com/artman/publish/article_1572.shtml

60. www.blacktalentnews.com/artman/publish/cat_index_33.shtml.

61. Terry Armour, "African American Films Ride the 'Cosby Effect,'" *Chicago Tribune, Nov 18, 2007.*

62. Ibid.

63. Ibid., www.chicagotribune.com/entertainment/chi1118_thisnov18,1, 3114830.story.

CHAPTER 9

1. "50 Years of Progress: Blacks in Politics 1951–2001," *Jet Magazine*, 2001, http://findarticles.com/p/articles/mi_m1355/is_22_100/ai_80162969/print

2. Nancy Bonvillain, *Cultural Anthropology.* Upper Saddle River, NJ: Prentice Hall, 2005, 312.

3. Rickey Hill, "The Study of Black Politics: Notes on Rethinking the Paradigm," in *Black Politics and Black Political Behavior: A Linkage Analysis*, ed. by Hanes Walton, Jr. Westport, CT: Praeger Publishers, 1994: 11–17.

4. Ibid., 11.

5. John Hope Franklin and Alfred Moss, Jr., *From Slavery to Freedom: A History of Negro Americans,* 6th ed. New York: Alfred A. Knopf, 1988.

6. Hill, "Study," 13.

7. "50 Years of Progress: Blacks in Politics 1951–2001," http://findarticles .com/p/articles/mi_m1355is_22_100/ai_80162969/print.

8. Sheila Harmon-Martin, "Black Women in Politics: A Research Note," in *Black Politics and Black Political Behavior: A Linkage Analysis*, ed. by Hanes Walton, Jr. Westport, CT: Praeger Publishers, 1994: 209–217.

9. Ibid., 210.

10. Ibid., 210.

11. Ibid., 212.

12. S. J. Carroll and W. Strimling. "Black Women's Routes to Elective Offices," in *Women's Routes to Elective Office: A Comparison with Men's*. New Brunswick, N.J.: Center for the American Women and Politics, 1983.

13. Harmon-Martin, "Black Women," 213.

14. Ibid., 213.

15. Sindya Bhanoo, "The New Black Brigade: Today's African American Politicians Have an Energy All Their Own," *Berkeley Journalism*, November 3, 2006; http://journalism.berkeley.edu/projects/election2006/11/the_new_black_brigade_today; J. Douglas Allen-Taylor, "Undercurrents: Those Who Get Caught in the Back Wash of Past Discrimination" *Berkeley Daily Planet*, October 19, 2007, http://www.berkeleydailyplanet.com/article1.cfm?archiveDate=10-19-07&storyID=28262.

16. Benjamin Wallace-Wells, "The Great Black Hope: What's Riding on Barack Obama?" *Washington Monthly*, November 2004, http://www.washington monthly.com/features/2004/0411.wallace-wells.html.

17. Wikipedia.org (http://en.wikipedia.org/wiki/Barack_Obama) 2007.

18. Eugene Robinson. "The Moment for This Messenger?" *Washington Post*, March 13, 2007. http://www.washingtonpost.com/wp-kyn/content/article/2007/03/12/AR2007031200983.html.

19. Wikipedia.org 2007. http://enwikipedia.org/wiki/Condoleeza_Rice.

20. Stan Correy. Condoleezza, Condoleezza. Australian Broadcasting Corporation's Radio National, April 3, 2005.

21. Wikipedia. Org 2007. http://enwikipedia.org/wiki/Condoleeza Rice

22. Eugene Robinson, "What Rice Can't See," *The Washington Post*, October 25, 2005.

23. "Condoleezza's Crimes," *The Black Commentator*, April 1, 2004.

CHAPTER 10

1. P. McClaine, N. Carter, V. DeFrancesco, M. Lyle, J. Grynaviski, S. Nunnally, T. Scotto, J. Kendrick, G. Lackey, and K. Cotton, "Racial Distancing in a Southern City: Latino Immigrants' Views of Black Americans," *The Journal of Politics* 68 (2006): 571–584.

2. U. S. Census Bureau, *Census of Population*, http://factfinder.census.gov/servlett/QTTable, 2002a; U. S. Census Bureau, *Redistricting File*, http://censtats.census.gov/data/NC/16037/9000.pdf, 2002b.

3. McClaine et al., "Racial," 576.

4. Ibid., 577.

5. Ibid., 578.

6. Ibid.

7. Ibid.

8. Black Travels.com, www.blacktravels.com/aboutus.html.

9. Ibid., Message Board, http://www.blacktravels.com/ireland_Dwilson.html, unedited.

10. Ibid., Message Board, http://www.blacktravels.com/musicofJAPAN_RoderickRoss.html, unedited.

11. Café de la Soul, http://cafedelasoul.com/#/aboutus/4520259484.

12. Café de la Soul, http://www.cafedelasoul.com/french.htm, unedited.

13. Yahoo.com, "How are African Americans Viewed by Other Nations," http://answers.yahoo.com/question/index?qid=20060630002129AAAtFUE.

14. Yahoo.com, "Yahoo! Answers," http://answers.yahoo.com/question/index?qid=20060630002129AAAtFuE, unedited.

15. Ibid., unedited.

16. Clarence Lusane, *Race in the Global Era: African Americans at the Millennium*. Boston: South End Press, 1997: 100.

CHAPTER 11

1. Eric Bailey, *Food Choice and Obesity in Black America: Creating a New Cultural Diet*. Westport, CT: Praeger Publishers, 2006.

2. Walter Greene. "Off the Runway: Lack of Black Models Brought to the Forefront," *Sister 2 Sister Magazine*, December 2007, 24–26, http://www.s2smagazine.com

3. Ibid, 26

4. Ibid.

5. Barbara Summers, *Skin Deep: Inside the World of Black Fashion Models*. New York: Amistad, 1998; Barbara Summers, *Black and Beautiful: How Women of Color Changed the Fashion Industry*. New York: Amistad, 2001.

6. Walter Greene. Off the Runway: Lack of Black Models Brought to the Forefront," *Sister 2 Sister Magazine*, December 2007, 24–26, http://www.s2smagazine.com

7. Procter & Gamble, "My Black is Beautiful," 2007, http://www.myblackisbeautiful.com/home.html.

8. Ibid., home page.

9. Dove Corporation, "Campaign for Real Beauty," 2007, http://www.campaignforrealbeauty.com/press.asp?id=4563&length=short&section=news

10. Ibid., http://www.campaignforrealbeauty.com/press.asp?id=4563&length=short&section=news

11. Eric J. Bailey, "Black America Body Beautiful," 2008, http://www.blackamericabodybeautiful.com.

12. W. E. B. Du Bois, *The Souls of Black Folk*. New York: Barnes and Nobles Books, 2003: 9.

SELECTED BIBLIOGRAPHY

CHAPTER 2

Altabe, M. and Keisha-Gaye O'Garo. Hispanic Body Images. In *Body Image: A Handbook of Theory, Research and Clinical Practice*, ed. T. Cash and T. Pruzinsky, 250–256. New York: The Guilford Press, 2002.

Barnett, H., P. Keel, and C. Grilo. Eating and Body Image Disturbances in Adolescent Psychiatric Inpatients: Gender and Ethnicity Patterns. *International Journal of Eating Disorders* 32(2002): 335–343.

George, V. and P. Johnson. Weight Loss Behaviors and Smoking in College Students of Diverse Ethnicity. *American Journal of Health Behavior* 25(2001): 115–124.

Jackson, Linda. Physical Attractiveness: A Sociocultural Perspective. In *Body Image: A Handbook of Theory, Research and Clinical Practice*, ed. T. Cash and T. Pruzinsky, 13–21. New York: The Guilford Press, 2002.

Kawamura, Kathleen. Asian American Body Images. In *Body Image: A Handbook of Theory, Research and Clinical Practice*, ed. T. Cash and T. Pruzinsky, 243–249. New York: The Guilford Press, 2002.

Mrozek, Donald. Sports in American Life: From National Health to Personal Fulfillment, 1890–1940. In *Fitness in American Culture*, ed. Katherine Glover, 18–46. Amherst: The University of Massachusetts Press, 1989.

CHAPTER 3

Bailey, Eric. "The New Black Cultural Diet," www.newblackculturaldiet.com.

CHAPTER 4

Bailey, Eric. *Medical Anthropology and African American Health*. Westport, CT: Bergin & Garvey, 2002.

CHAPTER 5

Ebony Fashion Fair Magazine, Fall 2007. See also their Web site, http://ebony fashionfair.com.

Summers, Barbara. *Skin Deep: Inside the World of Black Fashion Models*. New York: Amistad, 1998.

Vibe Vixen. 2006. Tracee Ellis Ross: Why Our Favorite Girlfriend Rocks! Fall Edition.

CHAPTER 8

Hunt, Darnell, Black Content, White Control. In *Channeling Blackness: Studies on Television and Race in America,* ed. Darnell Hunt. New York: Oxford University Press, 2005, 267–302.

CHAPTER 11

Bailey, Eric. *Fieldwork at The 50th Annual Ebony Fashion Fair at North Carolina A&T University, Harrison Auditorium,* Greensboro, North Carolina. November 3, 2007.

Ebony Fashion Fair Magazine. "Defining Fabulous: Celebrating 50 Years of the Ebony Fashion Fair." Chicago: A Johnson Publication. Fall 2007 edition.

INDEX

Africa, 14
African Americans
    athletes and fitness, 78–81
    body images, 1, 12, 24
    body types, 1, 49
    fashions, historical, 50–53
    female bodies, 5. *See also* Fitness
        industry
    female celebrities, unstereotypical,
        65–69
    global perspectives of, 117–123
    health and fitness books and,
        77–78.
    men's bodies, 4. *See also* Fitness
        industry
    in politics, current images, 114–115
    and sociocultural, historical, and
        political events, 107–114
    spending patterns, 63
    women in politics, 111–114
Alaska Natives
    defined, 14
    enculturation to preferred body
        images, 21
American Indians, 9, 14
American mainstream health and
    fitness clubs, 75–76
American mainstream society, 37
Americans, Central and South, 17

America's Next Top Model, 4. *See also*
    Banks, Tyra
Amos 'n Andy Show, 85–86. *See also*
    Television, African American
    image
Aniston, Jennifer, 5
Apple Bottoms, 3. *See also* Clothing
    industry; Nelly
Asian Americans
    body images of, 9
    defined, 14
    enculturation to preferred body
        images, 18
Asian Indians, 18
Atlas, Charles, 16
Aunt Jemima, 38

Bailey, Eric, 129. *See also* Black Amer-
    ica Body Beautiful Web site
Baker, Josephine, 53
Bally Total Fitness, 76. *See also* Ameri-
    can mainstream health and fitness
    clubs
Banks, Tyra, 4, 11, 56
Beauty pageants and contests, 44–46
Berry, Halle, 5
Black, defined, 14
Black America Body Beautiful Web
    site, 129–130

Black Entertainment Network, 130
Black Men of America, 11
Blackness, 35
Black Travels.com
  (www.blacktravels.com), 119–121
Blair, Billy, 54
Body image
  in college, 30
  in elementary school, 25
  enculturation of preferred, 12
  European American preferred,
    14–17
  historical review of preferred, 35
  in middle and high school, 28
  among professional adults, 31
Books
  African American health and fitness,
    77–78
  new American mainstream health
    and fitness, 73–75
Burton, LeVar 88. *See also Roots*;
  Television and the African American image

Café de la Soul
  (www.cafedelasoul.com),
  119–121
Cambodians, 18
Campaign for Real Beauty, 128–129
Campbell, Naomi, 4, 55, 127
CBS, 10
Chamorro, 18
Chinese, 18
Chinn, Alva, 54
Cleveland, Pat, 54
Clothing industry, 3
Collins, Jada, 127. *See also* Ebony
  Fashion Fair
Cosby Show, The, 88, 121. *See also*
  Television and the African Ameri-
  can image
Cuban Americans, 17
Curves, 75

Darden, Norma Jean, 54
Dash, Charlene, 54
Davis, Vernon, 81–82. *See also* Under-
  Armour

DeVore, Ophelia, 4
Dove, 1, 128
Du Bois, W.E.B., 131–132

Ebony Fashion Fair, 58–60, 127. *See
  also* Johnson, Eunice
Enculturation, 12
European Americans
  images in mainstream society,
    37–40
  and preferences for body images
    and types, 9, 13, 17

Fashion modeling industry, 4
Faulk, Marshall, 83
Filipino, body image preferences, 18
Fitness, 24-hour. *See* American main-
  stream health and fitness clubs
Fitness industry, 4. *See also* African
  Americans
Fitness Magazine, 5
*Food Choice and Obesity in Black
  America: Creating a New
  Cultural Diet* (Bailey), 23, 125
Fox, Vivica 3

Garner, Jennifer, 5
Good Times, 87. *See also* Television
  and the African American image
Green, Nancy, 38
Greensboro, North Carolina, 127. *See
  also* Ebony Fashion Fair
Grimes, MaDonna, 77–78. *See also*
  Books, African American health
  and fitness

Hair, 40
Hardison, Bethann, 54, 126–127
Harvard University, 131. *See also*
  Du Bois, W. E. B.
Hawaiians, 18
Healthiness, flexible cultural definition
  of, 25
Heber, David, 5, 74–75. *See also* Fit-
  ness industry
Hemsley, Sherman, 83, 103. *See also*
  Jefferson, George
Hepburn, Audrey, 15

Hispanics
   defined, 14
   enculturation to preferred body
     images, 17
Historically Black Colleges and
   Universities (HBCUs), 130
Hmong, 18
Horne, Lena, 53, 100
Hunt, Darnell, 84–90

I Spy, 87. *See also* Television and the
   African American image
Iman, 55, 127
Imus, Don, 9–10. *See also* Race and
   body image

Jackson, Barbarie, 54
Jackson, Jesse, 10, 109
Japanese, 18
Jefferson, George, 83, 103. *See also*
   Hemsley, Sherman
Jeffersons, The, 87. *See also* Television
   and the African American image
JET Magazine, 58, 105
Jim Crow (dancing team), 39
Johnson, Beverly, 55
Johnson, Earvin Magic, 76
Johnson, Eunice, 59. *See also* Ebony
   Fashion Fair 58–60
Jolie, Angelina, 5
Julia, 87. *See also* Television and the
   African American image

Keckly, Elizabeth, 53. *See also* Main-
   stream society's fashion industry
Kelly, Grace, 15
Keys, Alicia 3
King, Regina 102–103
Koreans, 18

Laotians, 18
L.A. Shape Diet, 5, 74–75. *See also*
   Fitness industry; Heber, David
Latifah, Queen, 66–68
Latino Americans
   defined, 8
   enculturation to preferred body
     images, 17

Lee, Spike 100–101. *See also* Movies
   and the African American image
Living Single, 90. *See also* Television
   and the African American image
Lopez, Jennifer, 5
Lowe, Anne Cole 53
Lundgren, Dolph, 17

Mainstream society's fashion industry,
   53–58
Maxwell, Daphne, 55
McDaniel, Hattie, 99–100. *See also*
   Movies and the African American
   image
McGuirk, Bernard, 10
McQueen, Butterfly, 99. *See also*
   Movies and the African American
   image
Melanesians, 18
Mexican Americans, 17
Micheaux, Oscar, 98–99. *See also*
   Movies and the African American
   image
Micronesians, 18
Mo'Nique, 66
Monroe, Marilyn, 11
Moonves, Leslie, 10
Movies and the African American
   image, 97–101
MSNBC, 10
Murphy, Eddie, 83, 101
Muscle Mechanics, 74. *See also* Books,
   new American mainstream health
   and fitness, 73–75
Muscle & Fitness, 82. *See also*
   Wallace, Ben
Music videos and the African Ameri-
   can women's image, 90–97
My Black is Beautiful campaign, 128

National Association for the Advance-
   ment of Colored People
   (NAACP), 86
National Black Feminist Organization,
   87
Native Americans, enculturation to
   preferred body images, 21
Native Hawaiians, 14

Negro Baseball Leagues, 130
Nelly (rapper), 3
Nike, 1
North Carolina A&T University, 127

Obama, Barack, 114–115. *See also*
    African Americans, in politics,
    current images, 114–115
OMB (U.S. Office of Management and
    Budget), Directive 15, 14
O'Neal, Shaquille, 76

Pacific Islander, 14
Pacific Islanders, enculturation to pre-
    ferred body images, 18
People Magazine, 11. *See also* Banks,
    Tyra
Perry, Tyler, 102
Podcasting, 23
Poitier, Sidney, 100. *See also* Movies
    and the African American image
Politics, Black, traditional image of,
    106–107
Polynesians, 18
Positive Advertising Campaign, 64–65
Procter and Gamble, 128
Puerto Ricans, 17

Race
    and body image, 7
    defined, 8
Rashad, Felicia, 88. *See also Cosby
    Show, The*; Television and the
    African American image
Rice, Condoleezza, 115. *See also*
    African Americans, in politics,
    current images
Robeson, Paul, 98–99. *See also* Movies
    and the African American image
Roots, 88. *See also* Burton, LeVar;
    Television and the African Ameri-
    can image
Ross, Tracee Ellis, 57–58
Russell, Jane, 15
Rutgers, women's basketball team, 10

Sambo, 39
Samoans, 18

Sanford and Son, 87. *See also* Televi-
    sion and the African American
    image
Saunders, Ramona, 54
Schwarzenegger, Arnold, 17
Shape Fx Jeans, 3
Sharpton, Al, 10
Simmons, Kimora Lee, 57
Simpson, Jessica, 5
Sims, Naomi, 55
Slim Down Sister, 77. *See also* Books,
    African American health and
    fitness
Souls of Black Folk, The (Du Bois)
    131–132
Spiegel, 3
Summers, Barbara, 4, 100, 126. *See
    also* Fashion modeling industry
Symone, Raven, 66–67

Taiwanese, 19
Television and the African American
    image, 84–90
Thais, 18
Tita-Reid, Najoh, 128. *See also* My
    Black is Beautiful
Turner, Lana, 15
TV One, 130
Twiggy, 15
Tyra Banks Show, The, 4, 12. *See also*
    Banks, Tyra

UCLA Center for Human Nutrition, 5.
    See also Fitness industry
UnderArmour, 81–82. *See also* Davis,
    Vernon
U.S. Office of Management and Bud-
    get, Directive 15, 14

Van Damme, Jean-Claude, 17
Versailles, France, 53–54
Vietnamese, 18

Walker, Madame C.J., 40–43, 130
Wallace, Ben, 82. *See also Muscle &
    Fitness*
Warsuma, Amina, 54
Washington, Denzel, 101–102

Whites, 14

Williams, Serena, 79–80. *See also* African Americans, athletes and fitness

Williams, Vanessa, 56

Williams, Venus, 79. *See also* African Americans, athletes and fitness

Winfrey, Oprah, 66–69

Winfrey's Favorite Things: Holiday 2004, 3

Woods, Tiger, 80–81. *See also* African Americans, athletes and fitness

Yahoo.com, 119–122

About the Author

ERIC J. BAILEY, PhD, MPH, is Professor of Anthropology and Family Medicine, and Medical Anthropologist, at East Carolina University. He has served as Health Scientist Administrator at the National Institutes of Health, National Center on Minority Health and Health Disparities, and the National Cancer Institute. He completed a post-doctoral Fellowship at the Centers for Disease Control and Prevention, and Emory University's Rollins School of Public Health. In earlier roles, he served as Program Director for the Masters of Public Health Program in Urban Public Health at Charles R. Drew University of Medicine and Science, and as Assistant and Associate Professor at the University of Arkansas Medical Sciences, Indiana University at Indianapolis, and the University of Houston.